The 3:30 Life

Living By *DESIGN* Rather Than Default

ISBN: 9798367627404 (Paperback)

Bible quotations, unless otherwise noted, are taken from the Holy Bible, English Standard Version (ESV).
Authored by Steve Stenstrom.
Book design and layout by Aaron Dean Sauer.
Edited by Jon Ackerman.

Printed by Kindle Direct Publishing, in the United States of America.

First printing, October 2023.
www.the330life.com

For Jesus,
the Author of Life

CONTENTS

Section Two
The 3:30 Life Pyramid

The 3:30 Life

Living By *DESIGN* Rather Than Default

Introduction

Life.

It's an interesting word.

Life.

Life can be long, but it often feels short.

Life is full of potential, but with so many limitations.

Life is full of beauty, and also full of pain.

Life is surprising and predictable, adventurous and monotonous.

And whatever we mean when we say "life," we're all searching for it. Some days we search harder than others, but we're always searching for a quality of life that is fulfilling, meaningful, and significant.

So if you're like me, this reality raises any number of great questions:

> *What is my life's purpose?*
> *How do I know if I'm doing life right?*
> *How do I know if I'm experiencing the best quality of life possible?*
> *How much of it depends on God, and how much depends on me?*

This book will help answer these questions and more. Before we get to it, allow me to introduce myself.

Over the course of my life, I've discovered that I have three passions — three things that make my heart light up and that you'll hear me talk about throughout the book. First and foremost, I've loved Jesus since the day I first met Him. Next, I love my family beyond all other earthly relationships. Finally, I've loved the game of football further back than my mind allows me to remember. In this book, you'll see how those three are interwoven together repeatedly.

My early years were spent in Rochester, New York, where the Buffalo Bills were my team. As a boy, I wore my #12 Joe Ferguson jersey more often than I should have. He was their starting quarterback, and ever since I was very young I dreamt of wearing a jersey like that one day myself. When I was 8 years old, we moved to Dallas, and my quarterback heroes soon became Roger Staubach, Danny White, and Gary Hogeboom. Then in high school, I was inspired by men like Joe Montana, Troy Aikman, Randall Cunningham, and Dan Fouts. With each passing year, I felt what you might call a "gravitational pull" to become like them, and to play the same position they played.

In 1990, I was recruited to Stanford University, where I soon became the starting quarterback. That was a significant year for me because it was also the same year I met Jesus and began to follow Him for the very first time. In a moment I call "The Great Exchange," I went from darkness to light, from death to life, and from default to design.

I was selected by the Kansas City Chiefs in the fourth round of the 1995 NFL Draft, and went on to play for the next six seasons. Today, I coach and mentor young quarterbacks, and I can't wait to coach my grandchildren one day.

I love being a coach.

They say that if you want to know a person, then you should get to know their perspectives. If you want to know who I am, I'd tell you I still tend to see life from the perspective of someone looking through the facemask that's attached to my football helmet, and at the same time the perspective of someone who deeply desires to love and honor God with his whole life. The book you hold in your hands is a reflection of this perspective. It's something that's been growing in my life for more than 30 years now, and a book I began to write in my mind more than a decade ago.

As you read, my hope is that you'll hear my voice as "Coach." I recognize that I am who I am today because of the great coaches who have poured themselves into me. Both in football and in faith, I'm the byproduct of mentors and coaches who have helped me navigate the journey all along the way. This book will feel different from other books you've read, and that's because you'll feel challenged and encouraged in the same way a great coach relates to his or her athletes.

However, I'm not only a coach — I'm also a player. As a fellow player, I stand in the middle of everyone who reads about The 3:30 Life. The last thing I'd ever want to communicate to you — whether intentionally or unintentionally — is that I've somehow "arrived" at the Life we're discovering together. An arrival date is coming for each of us when we get to the end of our days ... but we're not there yet.

So do you need to be an athlete to benefit from this book? Absolutely not! The essence of a coach isn't confined to the world of athletics. There are business coaches, leadership coaches, and creativity coaches. A coach is any person who walks with us, and helps us become the best person we can be. We all have our heroes — those posters that hang on our walls — but it's our coaches who help get us there.

As you'll soon discover, this book is divided into two main sections. The first section establishes the foundation for everything that will follow in the second. It unveils the primary and eternal truths that invite us into a deep and rich conversation about a quality of life that's available to every one of us. It helps paint a picture of the real arena — the actual playing field — where life unfolds.

The second section introduces The 3:30 Life Pyramid. Here you'll find a framework for life that I've discovered and developed over the course of my walk with Jesus. Far beyond another Christian formula, this Pyramid helps us learn to put first things first, always inviting us to see — to really see — the heart of God in the middle of the days we've been given on this earth.

Your days won't look like my days and my days won't look like yours ... and that's by God's design. We're all unique, and the lives God invites us into were never meant to be a carbon copy. Our culture lures us into a compare-and-contrast mindset, where we learn to envy the lives of others who seem to be more happy, more attractive, and more successful. But not God. He invites us to break free from the toxic deception promised in the game of cultural comparison.

And that's because He literally broke the mold when He made you.

Listen to these words from Psalm 139 and consider the implications personally.

"For you formed my inward parts;
you knitted me together in my mother's womb.

"I praise you, for I am fearfully and wonderfully made.
Wonderful are your works;
my soul knows it very well.

"My frame was not hidden from you,
when I was being made in secret,
intricately woven in the depths of the earth.

"Your eyes saw my unformed substance;
in your book were written, every one of them,
the days that were formed for me,
when as yet there was none of them."

Psalm 139:13-16

I didn't just write this book to tell you my story, but to help you discover your own. My firm belief is that you are uniquely designed, and I hope this book will help you discover the story He wrote for your one-of-a-kind life.

So we're back to square one, and it bears repeating. Whatever we mean when we say "life," whatever *that* is, we're all searching for it. And I know — perhaps now more than ever — that the quality of a capital L "Life" is for Today, and also for That Day. It's abundant and eternal, and it's crystal clear to me that both are found in Jesus, and in Him alone.

So if you're ready to discover and encounter that quality of Life, then I'm ready to walk it out with you. I'm honored to be a part of this journey, and can't wait to see what God does next. Let's go!

SECTION ONE

The 3:30 Life Foundation

CHAPTER 1

The 3:30 Life

START HERE

SCAN TO WATCH

Living By *DESIGN* Rather Than Default

The day I met Bill Walsh changed the trajectory of my football career forever. It was January 1992, and Coach Walsh was hired by Stanford to be the new head football coach where I was a quarterback on the team.

It had been three years since Coach Walsh retired as head coach of the San Francisco 49ers, but anyone familiar with football knows that he's earned the right to be on the Mount Rushmore of all-time great NFL coaches. His 1993 induction into the Pro Football Hall of Fame puts an exclamation point on his impact in the game.

Beyond the winning seasons and the Super Bowl victories, Bill Walsh is most known in football circles for being the designer and architect of the West Coast Offense. While winning seasons and Super Bowls are recorded and remembered, a select few have come along and changed the landscape of the game as a whole. Coach's system of offensive football did just that, and the echo of his impact remains every week during football season as several variations of the West Coast system are still prevalent across the NFL.

By the time I met him on that day in 1992, I had spent two years in the "system" under other coaches, and had just completed my first season as Stanford's starting quarterback. I would spend all six of my pro football years in the West Coast Offense as well. But the three years I had with Coach Walsh as his starting QB, which were also his final seasons as a head coach at any level, stand out as trajectory-altering for me.

That's because when the "author" shows up it changes everything.

The Echo of John the Baptist

John the Baptist must have felt that way when Jesus appeared on the scene. John had heard about the Messiah, and was even living his life's calling to "prepare the way of the Lord" (Mark 1:3). But when the Author of the book showed up, it changed everything.

The change that John experienced is best described in a short, memorable statement. Speaking about Jesus, John said:

"He must increase, but I must decrease."

John 3:30

John had met the Author of the book, and because he had, those seven words poured out, almost as if he didn't even have to think about it. Those words have echoed throughout history and continue to shape the lives of Christ followers everywhere.

It's a Life By Design

The 3:30 Life is what happens when we meet the Author of the book. It's about who decreases, and Who increases. It is marked by the persistent and resolute commitment of all Christ followers to pursue a fully transformed life from the moment of salvation to the moment they stand before the Lord.

The 3:30 Life is when a listener becomes a follower, and when an observer becomes a participant. It's when we get out of the stands and onto the field. Simply put, it's the life we've been created for.

It's a Life that's Outlined for Us

When a family tragedy hit us in 1995, I was thrust into a moment of eternal perspective. The loss of my younger brother on the weekend I was drafted to the NFL forced some serious times of reflection. As my wife Lori and I stood in the kitchen of our Chicago home trying our best to process it together, the presence of God was there with us. It was a moment of heartbreak and clarity. We found ourselves asking two eternal questions:

"What are we doing here?"

"Are we living our lives for what matters most?"

While I was living out my childhood dream to play pro football, I had my entire world rocked suddenly and unexpectedly. If hindsight really is 20/20, then I realize now that what we experienced at that time was the tension we might experience in Psalm 90.

Psalm 90 is about perspective, and that perspective is what I most needed in that moment, but it's also what we all need most in every moment. It gives a voice to the proper perspective for anyone pursuing The 3:30 Life.

In verse 2 of Psalm 90, we're hit squarely with the reality of the infinite nature of God: "... from everlasting to everlasting, you are God."

Then in verse 10, we're confronted with the truth about our own finite nature. The psalmist even gives us a timestamp for our years on this earth: "The years of our life are seventy, or even by reason of strength eighty..."

And finally in verse 12, a prayerful plea emerges from the finite heart of someone who cannot possibly comprehend an infinite God: "So teach us to number our days that we may get a heart of wisdom."

An infinite God has breathed life into each of us for a finite amount of days, and we must learn how to number those days. And the absolute reality of our life's fragility should push us into living intentionally by design, not haphazardly by default. Therefore, the sooner we get our lives in line with our Creator, the more time we have to maximize every moment until we meet Him face to face.

It's the Only Life that Matters

So why is this important? Why should we learn to number our days? Why must we decrease at all, especially when it seems so counterintuitive to achieving our personal goals and dreams? The answer is simple. It's because one day you and I will stand before Jesus face to face. And on That Day, we'll be asked to give an account of our lives.

> And the absolute reality of our life's fragility should push us into living intentionally by design, not haphazardly by default.

The 3:30 Life prepares us for that precise moment, not filled with fear and dread, but with beauty and gratitude. This is the Life that happens when believers ask what will be of utmost importance on That Day, and then choose to live today in response to that answer.

It's a life of daily alignment and repositioning with an eternal perspective.

It's a life that is not content to merely hear about Jesus.

It's a life that doesn't offer any quick fix, but embraces a winding path into unknown places.

It's a life that's not for the faint of heart, but requires a counting of the cost beforehand.

It's a life that doesn't busy itself with rungs on ladders.

It's a life that's accessible to anyone, and challenging to everyone.

It's a life that's simple but not easy.

My invitation is for you to live this quality of life. And as you walk the journey together with those who are a few steps farther along, you'll be stretched to your limits and transformed to your core. What else would you expect to experience, after all?

Because when the Author of the book shows up, everything changes.

CHAPTER 2

The Increase

START HERE

SCAN TO WATCH

Living By *DESIGN* Rather Than Default

Quarterbacks are among the most highly critiqued and evaluated athletes in all of sports. The stat lines are seemingly endless, and depending on who you ask, the formula for success as a QB in the NFL is highly nuanced.

One measure that always rises to the top, in terms of importance, is completion percentage. It answers how many passes were attempted, and how many were completed. The math is both simple and revealing. While most quarterbacks these days can hurt defenses with their ability to scramble and run, a large part of what they're hired to do, and what will ultimately lead their team to success, is their ability to get the ball to their receivers through the air.

On several occasions, Coach Walsh would say to me, "Steve, we're a better team when the football is not in your hands." And while that comment would always get a good chuckle from anyone listening, he had a great point. He was reminding me that when I fulfilled my role on the team best, the people all around me would thrive as well, and we were much more likely to move the ball down the field and score.

For many years, I've repeatedly heard my good friend and quarterback expert Trent Dilfer tell young QBs who want to develop and play in college, or beyond, that they need to become "completion junkies."

OUR MEASURE OF SUCCESS

Completions come when we know the play, execute the play, and get the ball to the intended receiver. When it comes to success, the evaluation of our performance will be largely based on how well we do that very thing time and time again.

In a similar way, did you know there will be an evaluation of us when the game of life is over? The writers of Scripture talk about it, and the reality of that evaluation should guide our approach to life. There are defined measures that matter to the One who created us, and specific outcomes He intended when He designed us.

As we follow Jesus with purpose and intention, the completion percentage we achieve here on earth must be maximized, and that's because completing our life's work is of utmost importance.

Remember what Moses said in Psalm 90:12: "So teach us to number our days." Another translation says, "Teach us to realize the brevity of life." Why? So that we might gain a "heart of wisdom." A life of "wisdom" is characterized by the appropriate application of the right information repeatedly.

So if The 3:30 Life is the framework for a life that maximizes the percentage of completions along the way, then The Increase is ultimately our life's completion percentage, as defined by God.

> There are defined measures that matter to the One who created us, and specific outcomes He intended when He designed us.

While the verse has become a tee-shirt and a bumper sticker for many Christians, John 3:30 is far more than a short, pithy motto. "He must increase but I must decrease" was as natural as breathing for John the Baptist to declare at that moment, and at any moment. It was natural because his life up to that point was focused on fulfilling what he had been created to do, and that declaration was simply an acknowledgement of completion. The Increase of Christ was what was supposed to happen when John did his part. Jesus was making the headlines and John was allowed to see it and celebrate.

Pass attempted. Pass completed.

But there's one more important consideration around this concept of completion. Completion percentage becomes increasingly important and impressive as the number of attempts goes up. For a quarterback to be 3-for-3 or 5-for-6 is not nearly as impressive as one who goes 18-for-21 or 38-for-45.

The goal for us is to maximize our days by attempting and completing as many "passes" as possible. We're to take the gifts and resources entrusted to us, and invest them wisely during our lives in ways so that God's plans and purposes are maximized in and through us.

JESUS, JOHN, AND EVERYONE ELSE

We're all people who've been created to complete specific works, and believe it or not, this concept is a common theme we'll discover all throughout Scripture.

The evening before His crucifixion, Jesus postured Himself before God in prayer. He wasn't just talking to God, but rather pouring His heart out to the Father. The moment was sacred, emotive, and redemptive. As Jesus prayed, one of His statements seems to jump off the page. "I brought glory to you here on earth by *completing* the work you gave me to do" (John 17:4 NLT).

As the weight of His impending death pushed down into His soul, Jesus declared the glory that His Father would receive by completing the work He'd been given.

Long before that night ever happened, John the Baptist was busy completing the work *he'd* been given. And when the crowds wanted to declare John to be the Messiah, instead of Jesus, his response was always crystal clear: "As John was ***completing*** his work, he said: 'Who do you suppose I am? I am not the one you are looking for. But there is one coming after me whose sandals I am not worthy to untie'" (Acts 13:25 NIV). Declaring the identity of Jesus was a significant part of John completing the work he'd been given.

So what about all of us living today? Completing uniquely designed assignments isn't just a lofty concept for people written about in the New Testament. These men and women weren't meant to resemble statues we walk past in museums, but rather role models and examples for us all to follow. "Now finish the work, so that your eager willingness to do it may be matched by your ***completion*** of it, according to your means" (2 Corinthians 8:11 NIV). Paul is talking about a real-life, rock solid, sometimes messy reality that all Christ followers are invited into. Paul also writes at the end of the Book of Colossians, "Tell Archippus: 'See to it that you ***complete*** the ministry you have received in the Lord'" (Colossians 4:17 NIV). When we know Jesus, like Archippus, the Lord has ministry He's designed each of us to complete.

THE INCREASE OF JESUS

As a young father, I had the privilege of driving my kids to school every day. And if you're a parent, then you already know that the conversations that happen on the way to school can be quite interesting. One morning, my seventh-grade daughter Brooke and I were having a really good discussion.

She was asking my advice about some issues that were obviously on her heart. I gave her my best set of answers, trying to embrace love, knowledge, and wisdom in the moment as much as I was able. Just as the conversation was wrapping up, she thanked me, and walked onto her middle school campus. As I was driving away, I knew the truth about what had just happened. I didn't necessarily tell her the wrong things, but I also knew my words didn't connect all the dots for her that I had hoped.

Later that morning, as I was feeling the inadequacy of what had transpired earlier, I felt God speaking to me through one of my favorite authors, Oswald Chambers. It was a milestone teaching moment in my life, and I couldn't ignore what God was impressing upon my heart.

"Don't worry Steve. It's Me who needs to increase in Brooke's life, and you need to decrease. My voice is far more important in her life than yours is. It always has been. And that will never change."

That was the day the language of "The Increase" began to take hold in my life.

Stated plainly and simply, it's more important for people to have an experience with Jesus than to have an experience with me.

Or with you.

This is The Increase. It's a term that has become, for me, a compelling reality that captures what should be the everyday experience of Christ followers, and should provoke in us a sense of anticipation that we carry with us all day, every day. It's what happens when our hearts proclaim, "Lord, I just wanna get out of Your way, because it's way better when You show up."

What Now?

The remainder of the book is about learning how to reorient our lives around that single truth, so I encourage you to pause, take a deep breath, and exhale this simple statement...

**People need Jesus far more than they need me,
and that will never change.**

The Increase happens when that phrase becomes the innate, instinctual response to *everything* we experience, and in *every place* we experience it.

If this is starting to sound like the life you've been longing for, then I invite you to keep reading. What's ahead in the chapters that follow will become exactly what you need.

But before you leave this place and move onto what's next in your day, here's a simple prayer that might help express the desires stirring within you...

God, I recognize You as the Designer of my life, and all I want is to live in consistency with that design. Please help me to identify the work that You've given me, and then inspire and enable me all along the way, so that I may complete that work. I want to maximize my days on this earth and make them count for the sake of Your glory, not mine. May I get off the throne, and bow low before the eternal God who has been there all along.

In Jesus' Name, Amen

"He must increase, but I must decrease."

John the Baptist

CHAPTER 3

The Decrease

START HERE

SCAN TO WATCH

Living By *DESIGN* Rather Than Default

Ask any former professional athlete what they miss the most from their playing days, and a high percentage will tell you it's the environment of the locker room. A football locker room at the collegiate or pro level is a fascinating place. I'm sure the same is true in other sports, but I can only speak firsthand about the sport I played. The intersection of team cohesiveness and the uniqueness of each individual made for some of the greatest memories of my life.

I felt challenged in the locker room environment, but I also felt safe. Very safe. Safe to be myself, safe to say what was on my mind, and safe to really get to know my teammates, and to be known by them. Having a common ultimate goal that we all shared helped foster that kind of environment.

But with every good thing, there's always a lurking threat that desires to disrupt the good. And in my experience, the threat can always be whittled down to one word. This one small word — a word with only two letters — holds the potential to ruin a locker room, a season, and even an entire organization. The word?

Me.

It's not only a threat to sports teams. It's a threat to all of us. It's deeply entrenched in our culture. It's in the foundation of our politics, our families, and even our churches. It's our default mindset and approach to life that makes up the strands of our collective DNA. We cling to "Me" with everything we have, and we become acutely aware of its grip only when we're asked to release it.

But getting ME out of the way is the requirement to following Jesus with our whole lives.

This will be a difficult chapter for many. I say that from a place of empathy, not of judgment or superiority. You may even be tempted to quit reading after this. That's because we're not just talking about simple things that are spiritual. We're talking about spiritual necessities that are complex. You'll remember the central message of The Increase:

People need Jesus far more than they need me,
and that'll never change.

On any given day, those words will land in our hearts somewhere between a confident battle cry and a broken confession. But make no mistake — they MUST become, for all of us, as easy as inhaling and exhaling the air we breathe. That's The Increase.

However, the decrease of self is the other side of that same coin. We can't have one without the other. If Jesus is to *increase* in and through our lives, then the "Me" that's so deeply ingrained in us must *decrease*.

> But getting ME out of the way is the requirement to following Jesus with our whole lives.

THE FOLLOWING

At the heart of our decrease, you'll find an emphasis on how important it is for us to be following the right leader, in the right direction. We're all following something or someone, but that action of following doesn't mean we're headed in the right direction. That's the reason why following Jesus is so important in the lives of believers — because He's the only Leader who's sovereign, the only Leader who sees the past, present, and future. A life spent following Jesus is a life that's taught, modeled, and inspired in Scripture.

JESUS CALLS US — You'll remember the story of when Jesus called Peter to follow Him. Jesus looked at Peter (as well as his brother Andrew) and said the words they'd been wanting to hear their entire lives: "'Follow me, and I will make you fishers of men.' Immediately they left their nets and followed him" (Matthew 4:19-20). That's the longing of *our* hearts, too. How many of us have been waiting to hear Jesus say, "Follow Me, and I will make you _____," where that blank line is filled in by the One who created us with that unique design? We all want to be made into something that God desires for us, but we need to play a part in the daily fulfillment of it. As God is making us into something, we must always be following Jesus.

PAUL SHOWS US — The Apostle Paul models what it looks like for us to be a follower. In 1 Corinthians 11:1 (NIV), he tells believers, "Follow my example, as I follow the example of Christ." Paul is helping us see what any great leader already knows.

The best *leaders* are the best *followers*.

The greatest influence you'll ever have on the people around you will happen if you become the best follower. Will people follow you? Yes. No matter where you're going? Actually, yes. But for a Christ follower, whose very life is decreasing, people should only follow us to the extent that we're following Jesus. We need to be able to look at our friends, our spouse, our children, our coworkers, and our world and say, "Follow my example, as I follow the example of Christ."

A GREAT CLOUD INSPIRES US — In Hebrews 12, we read:

> *"Therefore, since we are surrounded by so great a cloud of witnesses, let us also lay aside every weight, and sin which clings so closely, and let us run with endurance the race that is set before us, looking to Jesus, the founder and perfecter of our faith, who for the joy that was set before him endured the cross, despising the shame, and is seated at the right hand of the throne of God."*

Hebrews 12:1-2

When I was in seminary, I remember studying this passage and writing a paper on it. I realized that this is a stadium metaphor, but unlike any stadium I've ever played in. Collegiate and professional stadiums are filled with people who don't belong on the field. That's not a judgment or critique. It's just a reality. But this passage paints a beautiful picture of a stadium that's packed full of people who've previously been on the field, and who are now cheering us on to run the race with perseverance, and to finish it as we fix our eyes on the prize at the end — Jesus Himself.

It's a calling from Jesus. It's modeled by Paul, and by many others. And it's inspired by a stadium full of people who've already run their unique race.

Conclusion

Have you ever considered the beautiful contradiction of knowing just how small you really are, and smiling about it? It's just so counterintuitive — I know. But getting out of the way so that God can show up actually becomes a little addictive. It draws us into wanting even more of the decrease than we experienced last time. And that's because the more we remove our own perceived importance from every interaction, in every relationship, in every moment, the more often we experience the fruitful and abundant life God has designed for us.

Pursuing a life of decrease is upside-down and counterintuitive. I get it. But it's impossible to build our lives around the greatness of God when, all the while, we make every effort to maintain our own grandeur in the mirror.

I encourage you to keep reading, refusing to allow any competing voice to whisper the aspiration of personal increase into your heart. I assure you — that pursuit will become a chasing after the wind until your dying day. Instead discover together with me how to position yourself (and the people around you) to experience God as He shows up in surprising and unexpected ways.

In ways we could never imagine.

CHAPTER 4

The Great Exchange

START HERE

SCAN TO WATCH

Living By *DESIGN* Rather Than Default

We all want a life that matters. It's true for me, and I know it's true for you as well. But sometimes, it's hard to know where to find it. What I've discovered in my journey is the life I'd always dreamed of began the day I chose to follow Jesus. And the transformational change that's taken place since then was set into motion by an exchange that happened that very day.

In the game of football, there are two people on the offense who touch the ball on *every* play — the center and the quarterback. The exchange of the ball from one set of hands to the other is the starting point of every offensive play. And the importance of the exchange is the reason Coach Walsh *never* called a shotgun formation. You see, in a shotgun formation, instead of the ball being transferred directly from the center's hand to the QB's hands, the ball must travel through the air for a short period of time. And the risk of the ball being in the air during that exchange was not a risk he was willing to take. As a result, every practice I had with Coach Walsh always began with a five-minute drill that involved me and the center practicing that all-important direct exchange.

What's true on a football field is multiplied exponentially when it comes to what's true in living The 3:30 Life. If we want to live *that* life — a life where Christ is increasing, and we are decreasing — then the starting point is an *exchange* that must take place. Because you and I don't just show up on the planet, ready to live that kind of life.

A *changed* life always begins with an *exchanged* life.

LIFE FOR LIFE

Ephesians 2 provides a rich and foundational understanding for much of our lives, and it starts with a reality that might take you by surprise:

"And you were dead in the trespasses and sins..."

Ephesians 2:1

According to Scripture, we may have been physically alive at our birth, but we were spiritually dead. It sounds harsh, but stay with me. In contrast to the popular version of Christianity that's told — that we're good people in need of help — the biblical narrative tells the story of dead people who are in need of something far greater.

What do dead people need the most? Dead people don't need more help. They don't need to become the best version of themselves. They don't need to just try harder or think positive thoughts. They don't need to attend church more, give more, or serve more. There's only one thing that spiritually dead people need.

They need life.

> What I've discovered in my journey is the life I'd always dreamed of began the day I chose to follow Jesus.

And that's exactly what God provides. It's hard for me to read the next part of Ephesians 2 and not feel like the most fortunate person alive:

"But God, being rich in mercy, because of the great love
with which he loved us, even when we were dead in our
trespasses, made us alive together with Christ—by grace you
have been saved—and raised us up with him and seated us
with him in the heavenly places in Christ Jesus..."

Ephesians 2:4-6

Apart from doing better things or becoming better people, God's limitless love and incomprehensible mercy gave us the only thing we really need. He gave us life. But not just any life.

He gave us the very life of Jesus. He made us alive with Christ, even while we were spiritually dead. We didn't just wake up.

We were raised up.

And that's the exchange we all need — Christ's life for our life. It's the first time we ever go from Me to He. It's a rebirth that becomes the starting point of The Following. It's where The 3:30 Life begins, because it's where Life begins. And it's for *all* people!

For me, this exchange took place in the Fall of 1990. I was at a table outside of the Student Union at Stanford University. I may have heard the aforementioned truths for years before, but I didn't recognize the need to respond until that day. It's when I went from death to Life, and it's where The Great Exchange happened for me. This was my moment of being reborn.

When was your rebirth moment? That's an easy question for some, but difficult for others. It can be difficult because it takes recall and reflection to go back and remember it. But if you push yourself to remember the location and the people ... where does your mind take you? To say, "I don't remember when I became a Christ follower; I just know it happened at some point," is to minimize the power of God's story through you. Your rebirth story is the most sacred thing about you, because you're the only one who has that version of it. It gives words and phrases to the indwelling of the Holy Spirit in you. It shows the evidence of an earthly deposit that guarantees a heavenly inheritance. I encourage you to go back and refresh yourself with the season, the sights, the setting, and the words you said to God. And then learn to tell the story of your rebirth for the sake of the world, and to the glory of God.

> Your rebirth story is the most sacred thing about you, because you're the only one who has that version of it.

Is This Your Moment?

As you're reading this, and trying to tell your own story of The Great Exchange, it may indeed be an impossible story to tell, simply because there hasn't yet been a rebirth moment in your life. It's easy for anyone to try to convince themselves that they're following Jesus just because their parents or grandparents did so, or because they live in a "Christian" nation. But while traditions of the Christian faith may be passed down through certain people and geographies, the life of Jesus can only be given to *us* from *Him*. It's HIS life He's offering, after all — so it makes sense that only He can give it. Sitting in a church week after week doesn't make us into a Christ follower any more than sitting in a garage makes us into a car.

In John 17, Jesus is praying for us. As He does so, His words remove any lingering questions about what it means to become alive with the Life He's offering:

> *"And this is eternal life, that they know you, the only true*
> *God, and Jesus Christ whom you have sent."*

John 17:3

Notice what Jesus did not say. He didn't say, "that they may know *about* You." We can know *about* another person without actually *knowing* them.

The problem for most people goes back to that two-letter word we discussed in the last section — the word "Me". You've likely heard the word "sin" thrown around in these discussions before, and no matter what images that word conjures up inside your mind, it always goes back to that same empty two-letter word.

In the Bible, sin is actually an archery term, and carries with it the message of shooting an arrow, but missing the mark. It's rooted in a false belief that I can live up to the standards of God (of hitting the mark), and that if I don't, then He'll give me a free pass anyway because He loves me. Do you really think we can just enter into the presence of an all-powerful, holy, and perfect God on our own merit? We can't even live up to our *own* self-proclaimed standards, let alone His.

Even though I played my final three collegiate years at Stanford for Coach Walsh, the head coach who originally recruited me to Stanford was Dennis Green. After two great years of playing under him, he had the opportunity to coach the Minnesota Vikings. I'll never forget the day I sat in Coach Green's office, and he told me he was offering me a scholarship to come play football there. Even though I was too young to understand the full implications of how that would impact my life, it quickly became evident to me that someone else would be paying for my experience. I was being grafted into the Stanford family, and would experience all of those benefits for the rest of my life. I played at Stanford, met my wife at Stanford, lived on the edge of the campus for 20 years, had two kids born in the Stanford hospital, and was eventually inducted into the Stanford Hall of Fame. All of that and more, but I had to say "yes" to Coach Green first.

In a much greater way, the Creator of the universe has paid for the Life you're *designed for*. But Me must be replaced by He. Knowing about Him must become actually knowing Him. Identifying as a "Christian" must become living as a Christ follower.

Scripture couldn't be more clear about the only starting point for Life. First John 5:12 says, "Whoever has the Son has life; whoever does not have the Son of God does not have life." There simply isn't a way to experience Life without Jesus.

> In a much greater way, the Creator of the universe has paid for the Life you're craving.

If this is all starting to make sense to you, and if you've never gone from Me to He, then this really is the moment where rebirth can become more than a talking point for you. If that's you and you're ready to commit the remainder of your life to following Jesus, I invite you to pray this prayer in the quietness of your heart...

Dear God, thank You for loving me, and for pursuing me all the days of my life. I fully acknowledge that I have pushed You away, and that I've lived my life apart from You. For this, I am truly sorry.

In this moment, I ask You to forgive my sins, and to restore me completely back to You — back into the Life I was created for.

Jesus — I believe that You are God, and that Your death paid for the death I deserve. I believe that You rose again on the third day in victory over death, and I now receive that Life in exchange for mine.

I will follow wherever You lead, and this moment will become the story of my rebirth — a story that will become a reflection of You for the world to see.

In Jesus' Name, Amen.

If those words authentically reflect the convictions you feel in your heart and the commitment you're prepared to make before God, the Bible says that all of heaven is celebrating right now! This will become the most defining moment of your life, because you just went from death to Life.

As you read the following words from 1 John, please read them slowly, more than once, and pay attention to what's being proclaimed here. Which words resonate with you? Let them pour over you, into you, and through you.

> *"Everyone who believes that Jesus is the Christ has been born*
> *of God, and everyone who loves the Father loves whoever has*
> *been born of him. By this we know that we love the children*
> *of God, when we love God and obey his commandments.*
> *For this is the love of God, that we keep his commandments.*
> *And his commandments are not burdensome. For everyone*
> *who has been born of God overcomes the world. And this is*
> *the victory that has overcome the world—our faith. Who is*
> *it that overcomes the world except the one who believes that*
> *Jesus is the Son of God?"*

1 John 5:1-5

We all want a life that matters. It's true for me, and I know it's true for you as well. But sometimes, it's hard to know where to find it. What you're discovering is that the life you've always dreamed of began the day you chose to follow Jesus.

And for many of you, that day is today.

CHAPTER 5

X's & O's

START HERE

SCAN TO WATCH

Living By *DESIGN* Rather Than Default

Winning. Whether you're an athlete, fan, or just a casual observer, most everyone wants to win. You may be someone who seeks victory in some grueling event that takes a lifetime of planning and preparation, or maybe simply making it through the day is winning enough for you, especially these days. If we take a bird's-eye view of our lives, we all want to know that our days, hours, and minutes really do have meaning. This type of significance is a more profound version of winning than any game.

Sometimes that pursuit feels so elusive, seemingly impossible to achieve, and so much like chasing after the wind. While those around us seem to win without even trying, our attempts can feel hollow, or shallow, or never fully realized. If we're really honest with ourselves, we can feel these paralyzing impossibilities at nearly every turn.

This is why I'm so excited about what's included in these next few pages. I, along with millions of others who have gone before me, have discovered that there's a Source for our deep desire for significance, and that Source is the eternal God who rules and reigns forever, and who's created all of us with the passion to live a life that really counts. But there's also a source that's constantly opposing us, which is identified in the Bible as Satan. And if a football field can represent an accurate metaphor for our lives, then the heart of the matter is this:

**The reason we often feel like we're running in
quicksand is because there's a defense on the field too.**

TWO END ZONES

Etched onto the margins of every football field are two end zones, and *only* two end zones. As a quarterback, my goal was to move the ball down the field and into the intended end zone, and I spent much of my life learning a playbook that would get our offense to do just that. It would be far too simplistic to metaphorically label one of the end zones "God" and the other end zone "Satan." Instead, in a very real and compelling way, one end zone can be labeled "He," with the other labeled "Me." This is, after all, the essence of The 3:30 Life.

And it's _that_ constant Me vs. He conflict
that best describes the true and epic battle that's
warring in all of us.

What's the goal of the adversary? It would be ridiculous for us to play the game as if there's no defense on the field, so it's vital that we know what the enemy is trying to accomplish. Jesus alone knows that answer. He knows Satan's habits, tendencies, and motivations for every movement he makes. In John's Gospel, Jesus seems to convey the words His followers most need to hear, and then speaks those words of absolute truth into our stories.

Into our elusive, hollow, and impossible stories...

"The thief comes only to steal and kill and destroy. I came
that they may have life and have it abundantly."

John 10:10

Jesus says that the enemy comes "only to." It's as if Jesus is declaring a binary truth here, because in His mind, there really are only two options. The enemy comes into our lives to steal, to kill, and to destroy. But the other option, on the other side of the field, is that Jesus comes to give us Life, and to see us live that Life to the fullest extent possible. The enemy comes to push us backward into a life of Me, but Jesus comes to invite us forward into the abundant life of He.

Just like the offensive and defensive players on the field, we're always moving in one direction or the other. No one can follow Jesus and, at the same time, remain in the same place. And even though the eternal and final outcome of the believer's life was settled at the moment of The Great Exchange, we will live out the remainder of our days as players on that field, and we'll do so with difficulty and victory, with passion and danger. There are both X's and O's on the field, after all.

So is the enemy just trying to make our lives difficult? Does he just want us to be miserable? He may be doing just that, but that's not his ultimate goal. Once The Great Exchange has occurred in our lives, his primary goal is to minimize the effectiveness of our life in God's Kingdom, and in the lives of those around us. And he'll do that by focusing our attention on Me. Plain and simple.

> It would be ridiculous for us to play the game as if there's no defense on the field, so it's vital that we know what the enemy is trying to accomplish.

We *must, must, must* see the truth about Satan. Nothing in our lives will make any sense without this core understanding. His goal is to lure Christ followers into adopting a life that's primarily focused on themselves.

**He's whispering lies in your direction, my friend, and
he's trying to convince you that the joy and peace
and contentment you're craving will happen if you just
focus a little more on the person you see in the mirror.**

But when we counter those lies with what we know about The 3:30 Life, we're drawn to remember the truth...

That it's a choice.

That it's two, and only two end zones.

That we're always moving toward one end zone or the other.

That there's an offense and a defense.

That we're being offered a false life that seems logical, or a real life that seems counterintuitive.

That it's Me or He.

ONE WHO IS GREATER

Jesus comes to give His followers something entirely different than a counterfeit life, like the one the world around us wants us to buy into. The world is defined by the cultural norms of our day, one full of worry and hurry. But He comes to give us a life that's overflowing with living water, bursting forth from the fountain of The Great Exchange.

He comes to give us the significance we've always dreamed of.

Paul reminds us in Galatians 5:1, "For freedom Christ has set us free." The full invitation of Christ's life is to throw off the shackles of Me, because real freedom is discovered in the Life of He.

But how do we do that? Really do that, I mean? Not just put on a show for people at church, or fake our way through difficult relationships with coworkers or classmates? If it's the life we all want, then why aren't more Christ followers seeing it played out in their families, or workplaces, or churches, or communities?

It's a difficult question with a simple answer, and we'll spend much of the next chapter exploring it. In short, it will require the divine work of the Holy Spirit. Here's how Paul puts it:

> *"Now the Lord is the Spirit, and where the Spirit of the Lord is, there is freedom. And we all, with unveiled face, beholding the glory of the Lord, are being transformed into the same image from one degree of glory to another. For this comes from the Lord who is the Spirit."*

2 Corinthians 3:17-18

The full invitation of Christ's life is to throw off the shackles of Me, because real freedom is discovered in the Life of He.

God is transforming us into His image, and He's doing it through His Spirit. His Spirit inspires us to charge the field, to fully know that we've been created to be in the middle of the action, and not on the sidelines anymore. And it's the same Spirit that shows us how beautiful a Life of He really is.

CONCLUSION

The Great Exchange has unlocked, for you, the gift of Life as God intended it, but there's also a journey that began with your very next breath. And because you'll be playing it out against the backdrop of the enemy, it'll take intentional and purposeful living on your part.

But take heart. Jesus is leading you, and a great cloud of witnesses is cheering you on. It's the race marked out FOR YOU. You'll need endurance, but I promise that there's joy set before you. As we'll soon discover, the Spirit of God is giving you the strength to run with perseverance, and to see your life from God's vantage point.

You were made for this. The offer is real and abundant Life.

Keep following.

CHAPTER 6

The Film Room

START HERE

SCAN TO WATCH

Living By *DESIGN* Rather Than Default

Ron Turner was the coach at Stanford who recruited me out of high school. After our years together in college, we were reunited in Chicago when I played for the Bears. It was early one season, and I was a backup to Erik Kramer, who was our starting quarterback. After practice on a Wednesday, Erik and I went into the film room to study our own offensive schemes, but also to study the defensive film from our upcoming opponent, the Tampa Bay Buccaneers.

It was starting to get late, and I noticed that Erik and I were the only two guys left. I decided to call it a night, so I told Erik I was leaving, and headed out of the facility. As I did, I passed Coach Turner in the hallway. He asked me where I was going, and I told him I was headed home for the night. I could tell that something didn't sit well with him in my response. Our history together helped me read his facial expressions, and just as I was beginning to respond, he told me something I'll never forget. He said, "Steve, in my own experience, the first one out the door is usually the first one out the door."

And there it was. He knew I hadn't spent enough time in the film room to be fully prepared for a victory over the Bucs. So I did a 180, and headed back in to watch some more.

As a football player, you can't ever spend too much time in the film room. Why? Because the film, recorded from the highest vantage point possible above the field, gives us a visual display of what's really happening on the field. In football, we had a saying: "The eye in the sky never lies," speaking specifically of the film we were watching. Any player can deny running the wrong route, or throwing to the wrong spot on the field. But in the film room, those excuses don't hold up, because the eye in the sky never lies.

Likewise, as we pursue The 3:30 Life, we really can't spend too much time in the film room — in time spent with the Lord — learning to see our lives through His eyes, and our circumstances from His vantage point. Elevation shapes our perspective, and whether it's from the vantage point of an airplane, or a camera recording film from the top of the stadium, it's simple...

The higher our perspective, the better we ultimately see.

Analyzing the Defense

In football, the film room provides us with an honest and unique understanding of the opposing team's defense. In the same way, as followers of Jesus, learning to see our lives from God's vantage point will help us see our opposition with clarity and perspective. We've already discussed the reality of our Enemy, but the purpose of the film room is to expose his tendencies and schemes. Here's what we know to be true:

The enemy's language is lying. In John 8:44, Jesus puts it bluntly: "When he lies, he speaks out of his own character, for he is a liar and the father of lies." Our enemy is intent on lying about the trajectory of our lives, about the certainty of God's faithfulness, and about the goodness of the Author Himself. He's speaking statements that, if we aren't careful, can move swiftly into the depths of our hearts:

"You don't have enough."

"You aren't enough."

"You're not doing enough."

If those statements are giving a voice to your own self-talk, then you're not alone. In an age where social media invites us to live in constant comparison with others, it's those three lies that scream louder and more consistently than ever before in history. As a result, Christ followers must learn to discern, as well as mitigate against, when and where we fall into this comparison trap, listening to the father of lies. Then, by the power of the Spirit, we resolutely refuse to allow ourselves to go to those places.

The enemy's objective is to minimize God's effectiveness in our lives. Even though his primary scheme is to never allow The Great Exchange to happen in the first place, when it does, his secondary scheme is designed to thwart us from the completion of God's assignments for our lives. Remember, the enemy wants us to default back into Me vs. He.

The enemy's schemes are hurry and worry. In one of Jesus' most powerful parables, He describes four soils into which a seed is planted. The seed represents the Word of God, and each soil represents the life that grows as a result. One of the soils has thorns growing through it, and Jesus' interpretation of this soil speaks volumes into the schemes of the Enemy.

> *"And others are the ones sown among thorns. They are those who hear the word, but the cares of the world and the deceitfulness of riches and the desires for other things enter in and choke the word, and it proves unfruitful."*

Mark 4:18-19

"The cares of the world and the deceitfulness of riches and the desires for other things" are how Jesus describes what we're all offered on the listener's side of the enemy's message. When our focus is blurred by the false concerns that hurry and worry give voice to, the Increase of Jesus in our lives is diminished. The thorns will choke us, and they'll do so by always focusing on Me. They're always whining and demanding that we answer, "How do I get more? And more? And more?"

Analyzing the defense can get discouraging, and I know that from experience. But I also know as a QB that being in the film room will help me better execute my offensive assignments, so that we can overcome the defense.

> When our focus is blurred by the false concerns that hurry and worry give voice to, the Increase of Jesus in our lives is diminished.

EXECUTING THE OFFENSE

The film room allows us to execute the offense by helping us evaluate where we've succeeded, and also to assess where we need to get better. In life, as we're learning to number our days, we begin asking ourselves if we're engaging wholeheartedly in the work God's given us to complete. Having an offensive mindset allows us to take a proactive approach to life rather than living reactively to whatever comes our way.

By bringing courage, boldness, and humility into our film session with God, we will be convicted and inspired to grow far beyond what we could conceive on our own. Engaging with Him in this manner can be difficult when He challenges us, but it is deeply rewarding, and ultimately far more fulfilling than anything the world apart from God has to offer. The essence of this endeavor is to receive the assignments God has prepared for us, and to align our actions with the completion of those assignments.

However, a word of caution is necessary. If we're striving to accomplish that work on our own strength, then we're creating a recipe for disaster. It's the Holy Spirit — God's indwelling presence in believers — that shapes and equips us to become the people He's created us to be, and to complete the work He's given us to accomplish. Paul's words speak clearly to his original hearers, and to us today:

> "For this reason I bow my knees before the Father, from whom every family in heaven and on earth is named, that according to the riches of his glory he may grant you to be strengthened with power through his Spirit in your inner being, so that Christ may dwell in your hearts through faith—that you, being rooted and grounded in love, may have strength to comprehend with all the saints what is the breadth and length and height and depth, and to know the love of Christ that surpasses knowledge, that you may be filled with all the fullness of God. Now to him who is able to do far more abundantly than all that we ask or think, according to the power at work within us, to him be glory in the church and in Christ Jesus throughout all generations, forever and ever. Amen."

Ephesians 3:14-21

It's His power accomplishing His purposes.

It's His Life in us completing His plans through us.

It's He living through Me.

It's Me reflecting He everywhere I go, and to everyone I meet.

Unfortunately, this might not be the version of Christianity you've been taught. Some have been told that we receive Christ's life by faith (The Great Exchange), but that everything after that is up to us — in *our* strength, and with *our* will. In Paul's letter to the Galatian church, he gets confrontational and bold about this misunderstanding:

> *"Let me ask you only this: Did you receive the Spirit by works of the law or by hearing with faith? Are you so foolish? Having begun by the Spirit, are you now being perfected by the flesh?"*

> Galatians 3:2-3

That's a question believers must wrestle with every day. After *beginning* by means of the Spirit, are you now trying to *finish* by means of the flesh? In other words, after receiving Christ's life in The Great Exchange by the Spirit, are we now trying to live that life without the Spirit, in our own power? It's a pull-yourself-up-by-your-bootstraps way of living that runs entirely opposite to The 3:30 Life. The Increase of Jesus cannot and will not ever be experienced when His power is removed from the equation. We're not only saved by faith, but we walk in faith, too.

Dear friends, the life God's given us is ALL a gift from His hand. We receive the gift continually, and we serve the Lord's purposes in our lives in accordance with it. We position ourselves as stewards, not owners. We view our lives as in-process, not one-and-done. We're in right standing with God because of His grace, and every step we take will flow because of that standing as His sons and daughters.

> Our enemy is intent on lying about the trajectory of our lives, about the certainty of God's faithfulness, and about the goodness of the Author Himself.

WHAT IS YOUR FILM REVEALING?

So as you sit and watch the film of your life from God's vantage point, what's being revealed there? Are you buying into the lies of the enemy — that you don't *have* enough, or you *aren't* enough, or you're not *doing* enough? Is he using hurry and worry to cause your primary focus to be on Me rather than He, leaving you feeling stuck and confused seemingly without explanation?

Or maybe your heart cries out to run hard toward the unique and amazing work you've been hardwired to complete, but you haven't been able to overcome the doubt that blocks your progress. Perhaps you've drifted into a life of personal striving that's entirely devoid of the Holy Spirit's power and sustenance?

My invitation is to pause, to sit down, to take a breath, and to be entirely honest before God. As you lay aside striving, accolades, and masks, I invite you to pray something like this...

Jesus, I surrender. Again. Reveal to me the ways the enemy is causing me to turn my face away from You, and into the mirror focusing on me. Bring me back into a clear vision of the person You've created in me, and into the work You're inviting me to complete. May Your Spirit give me the strength and the power to move one step closer to completing it today, and every day after that. And continue teaching me how to get out of the way, and to stand in awe when You show up.

In Your Mighty Name I Pray, Amen.

As we close this chapter, if elevation truly shapes our perspective, then consider the words of Isaiah as they reveal the vantage point of the film room of God:

"For my thoughts are not your thoughts,
neither are your ways my ways, declares the Lord.
For as the heavens are higher than the earth,
so are my ways higher than your ways
and my thoughts than your thoughts."

Isaiah 55:8-9

SECTION TWO

The 3:30 Life Pyramid

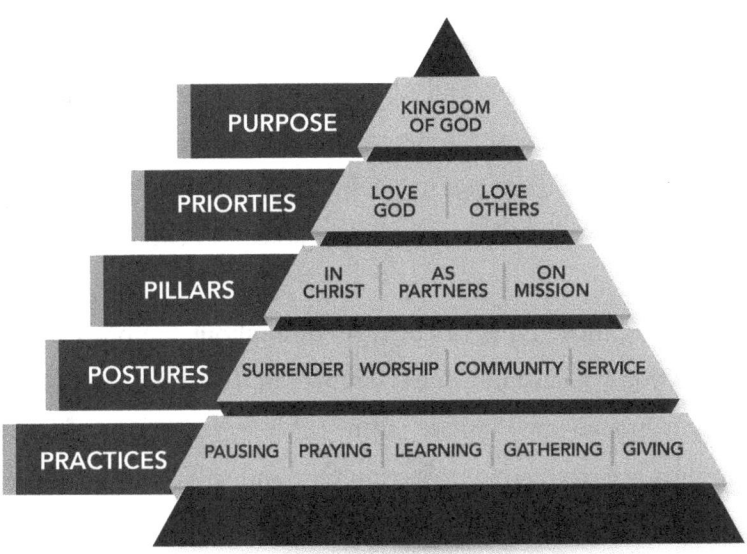

Section Two represents a notable and intentional turn in the book, and introduces The 3:30 Life Pyramid. Most pyramids start at the bottom and work their way up. This Pyramid, however, is the opposite, working its way from the top downward. As we discussed in Section One, the core of The 3:30 Life is the truth that God is the Initiator, and has come down in Jesus to meet us where we are. The 3:30 Life Pyramid is a reflection of this, and builds upon its unshakable reality. We all want our lives to count, and The 3:30 Life Pyramid is the most practical way I've discovered to help make that happen.

Coaches tend to think in terms of systems and paradigms, yet are careful not to slip into any specific formula that guarantees a desired outcome. They think in terms of having a proactive mindset, not a reactive one, striving to instruct others to operate by design, not by default. That perspective highlights why we need a framework like this pyramid, since most Christ followers don't have a strategic approach to following Jesus.

In Section One, I shared several stories from my football journey and the coaches who helped me along the way. I'll continue to do that here in Section Two, but there have been just as many, if not more, coaches in my faith journey who have walked with me and helped me understand life according to God's design. Similar to football, but far more important, the concepts and ideas conveyed to me by these coaches have informed my understanding of what it means to follow Jesus wholeheartedly.

You'll observe those types of concepts throughout the book as I try to convey to you what I hope you'll discover in The 3:30 Life and be able to apply it in your own unique journey. A very important example that you've already encountered in Section One and will continue to resurface in Section Two is the idea of living every "today" in light of "That Day." This perspective explodes off the pages of Scripture when we read it, and was ingrained in me by two men who have coached me in life as much as anyone, Jim Stump and Bob Shank.

Very early in my faith journey at Stanford I recall Jim regularly saying, "Steve, you're not ready to live until you're ready to die." And Bob's voice remains loud and clear in my mind, "There are only two days on God's calendar - Today and That Day. Not yesterday or tomorrow. Just Today and That Day." Taken together, I'm grateful for the perspective that has emerged over the course of my life in increasing measure to consider my final day on this earth - which will be my first one in His presence - and let it inform how I live each new day I'm given until then.

Paul says something similar in his first letter to the church at Corinth.

> "For no one can lay a foundation other than that which
> is laid, which is Jesus Christ. Now if anyone builds on the
> foundation with gold, silver, precious stones, wood, hay,

straw— each one's work will become manifest, for the Day
will disclose it, because it will be revealed by fire, and the fire
will test what sort of work each one has done. If the work that
anyone has built on the foundation survives, he will receive
a reward. If anyone's work is burned up, he will suffer loss,
though he himself will be saved, but only as through fire."

1 Corinthians 3:11-15

In Section One we focused on the only foundation which will unlock the potential for us to live every day according to God's design. Without receiving salvation by grace through faith in Jesus, nothing else matters. Once that is true of us, however, Paul's words above implore us to focus on life's finish line to gain clarity for the here and now. The "Day" or what I'm calling "That Day" is when we will see how we did in this life and how aligned with God's unique design we have lived out our "todays." The Day is coming when each of us will get to the end of our days, and we will see how we chose to live and what we chose to build our lives with when it is tested by God. Section Two is meant to help each of us build on the foundation using "gold, silver and costly stones" which will last rather than "wood, hay and straw" which will not when it is tested by the One who designed us to live for His great name and not our own.

So now, let's discover together the balance between living with intentionality, yet at the same time also following Jesus with open hands and surrendered hearts.

There's no better place to start that pursuit than with our Purpose.

CHAPTER 7

Purpose

START HERE

SCAN TO WATCH

Living By *DESIGN* Rather Than Default

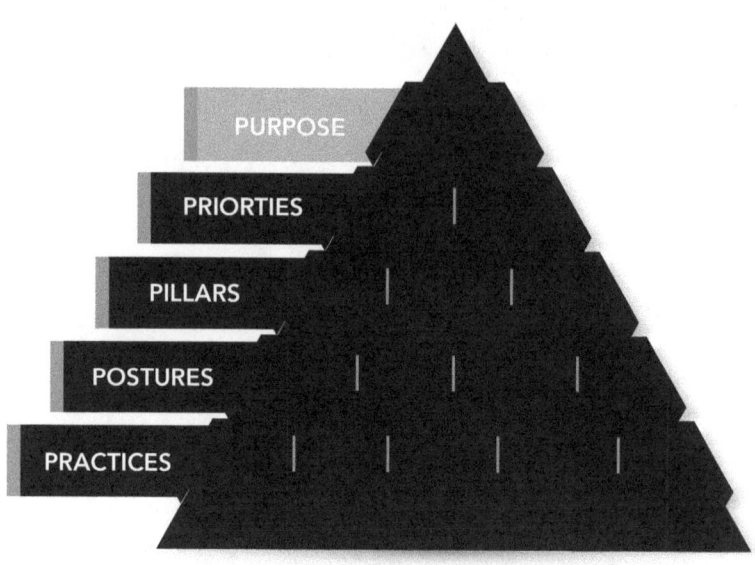

Everything up to this point in our 3:30 Life conversation has revolved around the bedrock reality that life as God designed it is meant to be about He, and not Me. As we've discussed The Increase, The Decrease, and The Great Exchange, we've landed on the firm foundation that living a full and abundant life requires Me to give way to He at all times, and in all ways.

So if that's the case, does it mean that Me is a bad thing? Something to be pushed away and tossed to the sidelines? The most obvious answer is found in the words of the Apostle Paul.

> *"Therefore, my beloved, as you have always obeyed, so now, not only as in my presence but much more in my absence, work out your own salvation with fear and trembling, for it is God who works in you, both to will and to work for his good pleasure."*

Philippians 2:12-13

Paul seems to be well aware that he has a responsibility to work *out* the salvation that God has worked *in*. That's what we are responsible for. At the same time, Paul knows that God will create outcomes that only He can do, in order to accomplish His purposes. That's what He is responsible for.

EVERYTHING HAS A PURPOSE

Purpose. We pursue it. We chase after it. We read books about it and register for conferences to help us discover it. We try our best to identify it in our own lives, and in the lives of the people we hold dear.

Webster defines purpose as "an end to be attained." Oxford defines it as "the reason for which ... something exists." You probably have your own working definition of "purpose," whether you can put it into words or not. Regardless, we'd all agree that everything has a purpose.

The glasses on our faces exist to help us see more clearly. The jackets we wear on cold days help keep us warm. The roads on which we drive, the cars we drive on those roads, and the multiple devices we use each day all have this one thing in common: They all have a specific and intended purpose. Their creator made them that way.

You were created for a purpose too, because your Creator made you that way.

While classes, conferences, books, and online courses might be immensely helpful in discovering the elements of your *uniqueness*, my belief is that discovering your *purpose* is actually much easier than that. It comes from looking outward, not inward. Only the Creator can tell the objects of His creation what their purpose is, and as followers of Jesus, our purpose is clear, simple, and to the point.

In the Gospel of Matthew, Jesus puts it into words that we can all understand. While we might believe that a more intricate and complex explanation is required, Jesus keeps it simple.

"But seek first the kingdom of God and his righteousness,
and all these things will be added to you."

Matthew 6:33

Our purpose is the Kingdom of God. We will discover more of what the Kingdom entails in the next chapter, but it's clearly meant to be the primary pursuit for anyone desiring to live in alignment with God's design.

My wife Lori and I launched a ministry in 2004 called Kingdom First Ministries. We wanted to make it clear in our name what our purpose was, and still is — to be Kingdom First people in all things. We were being consistent, but not revolutionary. We were simply echoing what the saints through the ages have known. The men and women who walked with Jesus on the desert sands understood it as well — that the purpose of their lives was to live in, and for, the Kingdom of God. It was Jesus' favorite topic to discuss and illustrate, and as His followers, we should take our cue from Him. So if it feels like we're taking a walk on sacred ground here, it's because we are!

WE ALL HAVE UNIQUE ROLES

If we all share the same Purpose — to live Kingdom First lives — then where does our uniqueness come into play? If we're to run the race that God has "set before us" (Hebrews 12:1), then where do we draw the line between the general and the specific? While our purpose as Christ followers is the same, the roles we individually play in His Kingdom are as different as the day is long.

Our unique roles are discovered within the context of our active relationship with Jesus, and they're revealed to us over time. Our roles are our assignments, the parts we play, and the works we're designed to walk into. They're a byproduct of that primary and intimate relationship with Jesus, and literally cannot exist apart from The Following. As we continue to walk in step with Jesus, we learn to see how we've been uniquely created — with certain passions and potentials — to pursue His Kingdom purposes in the world. Our assignments will come to us, over time, as He chooses to reveal them.

> We were being consistent, but not revolutionary.

JOHN'S EXAMPLE

John the Baptist's purpose was the Kingdom of God, and within that purpose his unique role was to prepare the way for the coming Messiah by pointing people toward Jesus, and away from himself. It's almost like John can't help but point and proclaim it's He, not Me, every time.

> *"John answered them, 'I baptize with water, but among you*
> *stands one you do not know, even he who comes after me,*
> *the strap of whose sandal I am not worthy to untie.' These*
> *things took place in Bethany across the Jordan, where John*
> *was baptizing. The next day he saw Jesus coming toward*
> *him, and said, 'Behold, the Lamb of God, who takes away*

the sin of the world! This is he of whom I said, "After me
comes a man who ranks before me, because he was before
me." I myself did not know him, but for this purpose I came
baptizing with water, that he might be revealed to Israel."

John 1:26-31

Did John complete his assignment from God? Absolutely. However, John's purpose, like ours, continues beyond our lives because the Kingdom of God transcends our lives. In other words, the purpose is not ours to complete, but the assignment is.

THE RIPPLE EFFECT

We've already highlighted the counterintuitive nature of The 3:30 Life, but there is perhaps no greater display of this nature than in the area of our purpose. If we want to live a life of purpose in the Kingdom of God, then we'll need to fully embrace the Ripple Effect.

We all know what happens when we throw a rock into a still pond. When the stone lands in the water, ripples automatically go out from the original landing point. There is no need to convince the water to ripple, nor is there any limitation placed on the rock. Ripples are the natural byproduct of a splash, because in God's created order, He made it that way. The same is true in His Kingdom. When we seek His Kingdom FIRST, then literally everything else is not ours to worry about.

But the Kingdom Ripple Effect carries with it some inherent confusion. It's simple, but it's not always clear. There seem to be two main areas where this lack of clarity often manifests itself: in our families, and in our jobs.

These two roles in life sometimes confuse and hijack our understanding of purpose, and can actually shift our eyes away from God's Kingdom, and onto something that might be noble, but inevitably lesser.

All of us are passionate about our families, as we should be. We say things like, "My family is my purpose," or "My number one priority in life is to be a great spouse." When we say or imply these things, we're actually swapping what's primary for what's secondary. Our families are a role we fulfill as a part of God's plans and purposes for our lives. They may be our assignment, our work, or the part we play, but our families are not our purpose. So while it's obviously important to love your spouse well, you need to prioritize loving Jesus first and foremost. He'll then show you how to go and love your spouse, and He'll help you do it by the power of His Spirit breathing His very life through you. That's the Ripple Effect.

> In other words, the purpose is not ours to complete, but the assignment is.

In a similar fashion, many of us have made the mistake of making our occupations and our purpose synonymous — at least in our hearts. My purpose in life was never to be a quarterback in the NFL or a ministry leader, but rather to live my life in God's Kingdom. Our jobs may be an assignment from God for us to fulfill, but they're not the primary purpose in life. So many well-intended people pour their entire understanding of God's purpose into their jobs, and expect a Kingdom-sized return at the end of the day, only to discover that their realized return simply can't satisfy them. We don't need to worry about climbing the corporate ladder. Instead, we need to serve God's

Kingdom purposes in our jobs, and allow Him to create the outcomes in us, and the people around us. That's the Ripple Effect.

These are important concepts and might present a new way of thinking, but purpose for Christ followers must remain a singular pursuit. Courage is needed to honestly ask ourselves if we've allowed our families or our occupations to rise to a place of preeminence in life. Like you, I've often struggled with the slippery slope of viewing my family and my profession as my purpose. But we cannot have two ultimate purposes without a battle ensuing between competing objectives. We'll seek to satisfy both and fail to satisfy either, because to live a life with competing purposes is to live a life God never intended. However, if we maintain a proper hierarchy — pursuing that which is preeminent in God's created order — then the Ripple Effect will impact the other areas we care about naturally, and will actually serve to reinforce the hierarchy itself.

CONCLUSION

We'll launch into the Kingdom of God next. But before we do, consider one of the most beautiful and accurate depictions of how the Apostle Paul experienced purpose.

"Not that I have already obtained this or am already
perfect, but I press on to make it my own, because Christ
Jesus has made me his own. Brothers, I do not consider
that I have made it my own. But one thing I do: forgetting
what lies behind and straining forward to what lies
ahead, I press on toward the goal for the prize of the
upward call of God in Christ Jesus."

Philippians 3:12-14

What a beautiful expression from the life of someone who isn't done yet, who refuses to stare in the rearview mirror, and who presses forward into a world where God reigns.

You want to know what direction you should go? Go forward into the Kingdom of God. If you're following Jesus, you'll be sure to get there, because that's always where He's headed. You don't have to search for the Kingdom of God. You simply need to follow Jesus, and let His splash create the ripple effects that become, for you, His moments of Increase. When we live Kingdom First lives, He'll show up in the places and spaces that we care about the most, and He'll do so in ways we couldn't have scripted on our best day.

This really is God's will, God's way. It's always His strength, not mine ... and in His timing, not mine. It depends entirely on He, not Me.

CHAPTER 8

The Kingdom of God

START HERE

SCAN TO WATCH

Living By *DESIGN* Rather Than Default

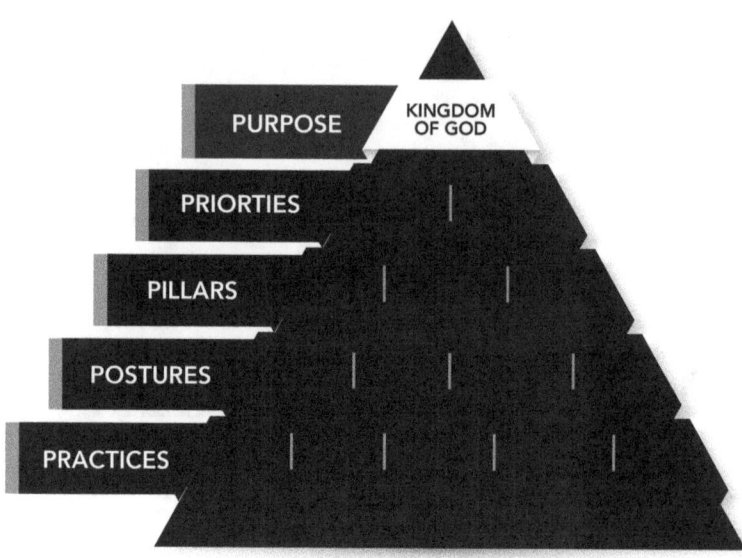

Whether in college or the NFL, I always loved game days. All game days. That being said, certain venues and certain opponents were a little extra special. When I played for Stanford, a Saturday in South Bend, Indiana, playing against the Fighting Irish of Notre Dame was the ultimate setting and foe. In 1992, we experienced one of the greatest football memories of my life in Notre Dame Stadium. We fell behind 16-0 early in the game to the sixth-ranked team in the nation, and came roaring back to win 33-16 against that perennial powerhouse.

So as you might expect, when we returned to play again there two years later, my expectations were high for another epic battle and potential victory. Suffice it to say a different outcome occurred, and a very different (but much more significant) defining moment unfolded right before my eyes.

Although we'd only trailed 10-3 at halftime, Notre Dame went on to score the first 24 points of the second half. With 13:56 remaining in the fourth quarter, and now trailing 34-3, Coach Walsh taught me a lesson that has impacted my life far more than I could have predicted at the time.

After yet another failed offensive series, Coach Walsh called us together and said, "Guys, we're making this way more complicated than we need to. On our next drive, I'm calling 22 Z-In for every play. I just want you guys to focus on executing your assignment and take whatever the defense gives you."

22 Z-In is a play that contains all the basic and foundational elements the West Coast Offense was built on. Everything that's made it thrive to this day is wrapped up inside of a play like 22 Z-In. While it might not seem like a big deal for many, for anyone who's played the game, they understand that Coach Walsh's new strategy was shocking for two fundamental reasons. First, it's unheard of for a great offensive mind like Bill Walsh to run the same play repeatedly over and over again. Secondly, it's striking that he chose a play like 22 Z-In because of its utterly basic and simplistic nature. At that moment, Coach could not have possibly chosen a play that was more elementary.

So even though it seemed crazy when he said it, for our next series we ran 22 Z-In for six straight plays, and drove right down the field and scored a touchdown. I'd love to say we came storming back after that and prevailed victorious, but that didn't happen. We ended up losing 34-15, but the long-term "win" has proven far sweeter in my life as the years have gone by.

As I reflect on that day, I realize Coach Walsh was teaching us a foundational lesson that would forever transform our effectiveness in the West Coast Offense. It was as if he wanted us to discover that the essence of the whole system was predicated on our understanding of *one basic play*. Years later I sat down with Coach Walsh to get his perspective on

22 Z-In, and try to confirm his intentions that day back in South Bend. Here's what he told me...

> "Our 22 Z-In was like a double play from the shortstop to the second baseman to the first baseman. I mean it was practice, practice, practice until we got it right because we wanted high consistency. It was a matter of running distinct patterns, splits, mechanics for the quarterback, progression, and basically not attempting to out-strategize ourselves."

And there it was — a glimpse into the mind of the author. In the course of that conversation, and ever since then, I'm convinced that Coach was trying to teach this: If you understand 22 Z-In, you'll be able to understand everything about what to do within the system. But, if you don't understand 22 Z-In, you won't really understand any of it.

In my walk with Jesus over the past 30-plus years, I've come to realize that He has regularly been trying to help me discover something about knowing Him that is equally foundational and far more significant.

It's what He called the Kingdom of God.

And like 22 Z-In, if we understand the Kingdom of God as Jesus revealed it, we'll be able to understand everything about how to live within that Kingdom.

> It was as if he wanted us to discover that the essence of the whole system was predicated on our understanding of *one basic play*.

What is the Kingdom of God?

Volumes have been written about the Kingdom of God. Depending on the Gospel writers, it might be referred to as "the Kingdom of God" or "the Kingdom of Heaven." In everyday life, it's best understood as the rule of God. But no matter what words describe it, we'll need to settle ourselves on the fact that it was the absolute center of Jesus' teaching.

The Kingdom was at the center of Jesus' teaching. Jesus came to reveal a new Kingdom reality for us, even though it wasn't a new reality for Him. He is the absolute and sovereign King over all, so it makes sense that the epicenter of Jesus' teaching would be about His Kingdom. Observers from diverse backgrounds listened intently as Jesus explained what this Kingdom was like, and watched as He ultimately died a gruesome death to make the way for all people to enter into it. These same people stood in amazement as they witnessed Him reclaim His place of authority and power when He was publicly raised from the dead by the power of God. If there was ever any thought that someone could challenge His authority or power — whether in heaven, on the earth, or under the earth — His life's ministry, His sacrificial death, and His jaw-dropping resurrection made any further challenge absurd.

The Kingdom is never fully defined by Jesus. While stories of the Kingdom flowed naturally from the King, He never really said, "Hey everyone. Let's huddle up. Here's exactly what the Kingdom of God is..." Instead, He was always helping people understand this Kingdom that was counterintuitive to them. Jesus would often begin His teachings with "The Kingdom of God is like..." and then He'd tell a story using a metaphor that His listeners could understand, like farming, bread, relationships, or money, just to name a few. He used things that we do know and understand to illuminate the things that are very difficult to know and understand. He drew our attention to God's Kingdom at every turn, and then illustrated it without defining it. And while this might be frustrating to some, Jesus knew He was inviting people into something that's best understood through stories, because there are some things that no human can create words for.

OUR LIVES IN THE KINGDOM OF GOD

And even though there are elements of God's Kingdom that can never be fully understood on this side of heaven, followers of Jesus can still learn to embrace a life of knowing about it, without knowing *everything* about it. For those who are discovering The 3:30 Life, there are certain elements of God's Kingdom that are more than clear, and revealed to us throughout the entirety of the New Testament. These truths are living and breathing principles for those who are hungry and thirsty for the abundant Life that Jesus promises.

> He used things that we do know and understand to illuminate the things that are very difficult to know and understand.

The King of the Kingdom is already talking about it. If it was His favorite and most important topic of discussion during His earthly ministry, then why would the risen Christ quit talking about it now? So if you want to understand the Kingdom, listen closely to what He's saying. Read the Gospels — especially Matthew, Mark, and Luke — and keep an eye out for Kingdom language. What's being said about it? What's being illustrated through the stories and parables of Jesus? What are the best and worst human responses to it? So, if He's still talking about it, we should listen.

The Kingdom of God is always where Jesus is going. The realm where God reigns is advancing and moving wherever Jesus is advancing and moving. So if you want to know where the Kingdom is, then follow Jesus into it, and do so each and every day. It's a Kingdom that unfolds as we listen, follow, and say "yes" to the opportunities He gives us, even when it doesn't seem to make perfect sense. So, if He's already going there, we should follow.

The Kingdom of God is naturally manifested in community. Here's the truth about the heart of Jesus: He already knows and fully appreciates that the Kingdom of Heaven is a really hard reality for any of us to understand. Given that difficulty, it's vital that we pursue this Kingdom alongside others who share the same vision. This is where we start to understand what it means to not just go to church, but to be immersed in a community as The Church. As God's people, we are better when we are together. So, if He's already establishing a community, we should participate.

The Kingdom of God is He, not Me. When we find ourselves living a life in the kingdom that's focused on *us*, about *our* rights and privileges, or about how *we* find success in life with a little help from Jesus, then we're confusing the Kingdom of God with one of our own making. The real Kingdom that Christ's original followers walked into recognizes that the King of the Kingdom is Jesus. It's always Jesus. They struggled with the same misunderstandings we do today, but they had a strong sense that the Savior they were following, into the Kingdom He was proclaiming, was the very same God who exists from everlasting to everlasting. When our lives are marked by He not Me, we're investing in something that has eternal potential, infinite value, and everlasting life. So, if it's already about His increase, we should decrease.

> It's a Kingdom that unfolds as we listen, follow, and say "yes" to the opportunities He gives us, even when it doesn't seem to make perfect sense.

Listen.

Follow.

Participate.

Decrease.

CONCLUSION

When the disciples asked Jesus how they should be praying, He quickly spoke about God's Kingdom. He said, "Your kingdom come, your will be done, on earth as it is in heaven" (Matthew 6:10). He told His original hearers, His followers today, and everyone in between to acknowledge the rule and reign of God, and to make a heartfelt appeal for it to happen on earth, just like it's already happening in heaven.

But that's where the tension lies, right? What we pray to see isn't always visible yet. What we long to experience isn't always happening, at least not yet. We see the Kingdom in part, but not fully. Even beyond seeing, we feel this tension deeply in our daily life where there's beauty and pain, victory and defeat, success and failure, joy and heartache. It's hard to be a foreigner in a strange land, after all, but that's exactly what we are as Christ followers. If you've ever traveled internationally, you know how uncomfortable it can feel. That's because our primary citizenship is in a different place. And while one day the Kingdom will come in all its fullness, at present we're living as people who see and feel that we're not at home. Has the enemy been defeated? Yes, and resolutely. Yet do we still feel like foreigners here? Yes, and understandably.

So take heart. The King of the Kingdom fully understands and empathizes with the tensions that are pulling on your heart and mind, manifesting themselves every day in your life. Every follower of Jesus has felt — to some extent — the desperate longings that you're feeling. It was perplexing to Christ's original followers, and it's still perplexing to us today.

But it happened. Jesus invaded earth with heaven. It was an inbreaking like we've never seen before. At the cross He asserted His power, disarming the enemy. In those days, when an army was defeated, they would be paraded through the streets, making a public spectacle of each and every one. Paul taps into this reality when he writes...

"And you, who were dead in your trespasses and the uncircumcision of your flesh, God made alive together with him, having forgiven us all our trespasses, by canceling the record of debt that stood against us with its legal demands. This he set aside, nailing it to the cross. He disarmed the rulers and authorities and put them to open shame, by triumphing over them in him."

Colossians 2:13-15

So I'll say it again: Take heart. You belong to the King of the Kingdom.

He is for you.

He is with you.

And He loves you.

His one Purpose must become ours too.

And if we understand the Kingdom of God as Jesus revealed it, we'll understand everything else.

CHAPTER 9

Priorities

START HERE

SCAN TO WATCH

Living By *DESIGN* Rather Than Default

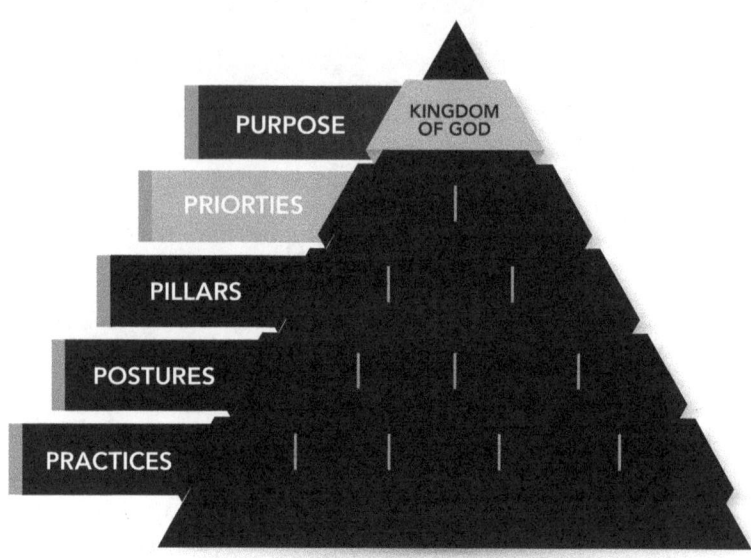

From the Increase of Jesus, to the Me to He transformation, to The Great Exchange, and into The Following, it might seem like we've traveled thousands of miles so far. And we have. But there's still a journey ahead of us — one where God is inviting us, leading us, and transforming us.

So if the purpose of our lives is the Kingdom of God, and if that Kingdom is best described as the realm where God reigns, then what should Christ followers *do* about it? There must be some practicality to all of this. You and I need to wake up every morning, and by the power of the Holy Spirit, we must *do something*. The pressing question becomes: How do we put into *action* everything we're learning?

The answer lies in our priorities, and as you may have already guessed, it's counterintuitive.

When I first joined the football team at Stanford, there were so many things that caught my eye. At the top of that list were the accomplishments of a previous Stanford quarterback named John Elway. His list of accolades was long and impressive, and every record-setting accomplishment had John's name next to it. Little did I know that four years later, the name next to the majority of those accomplishments would be changed from John's to mine.

That being said, I never concentrated on breaking Elway's records. That was never my focus or my priority. I never walked into a practice or a game and thought, "My focus here is to break John's records." Instead, my focus was on faithfully fulfilling my role as a quarterback. My priority was learning to become the best version of myself, for the sake of my team. And somewhere along the way, my numbers surpassed Elway's numbers, and my name replaced his name (and yes, other names have since replaced mine).

But accolades were never my priority.

Our priorities become our areas of focus. They're what we keep our eyes on, and what we lean into. Priorities inform everything we do. They guide the journey, regardless of where it leads. They're the fuel for a life that's being lived by *design*, not by *default*. Additionally, they help create a hierarchy of importance, giving us the freedom to live intentionally for whatever we place at the top of that hierarchy. Priorities strengthen our "yes" and reinforce our "no."

Sound important? That's because they are.

> There must be some practicality to all of this. You and I need to wake up every morning, and by the power of the Holy Spirit, we must *do something*.

Why are Priorities so Important?

Priorities give us focus. It's a beautiful thing for a Christ follower to wake up every new day and, even though they may not know where Jesus is taking them, they know with certainty what they should be focusing on during that day — during their unique Following. The right priorities focus our actions on the true and best things. They provide us with God's True North when we are desperately needing direction. They allow us to live all of our "todays" in the light of That Day when we ultimately see the Lord face to face. Our priorities prompt us to begin with the end in mind, teaching us (and reteaching us) to "number our days that we may get a heart of wisdom" (Psalm 90:12).

Priorities unify us beyond our preferences. As followers of Jesus, we all have a unique laundry list of personal preferences. Whether it's food, clothing style, or church denomination, our preferences help us define what's important to us. This all sounds simple enough, until we're asked by Jesus to live in unity with one another. How can we become unified when our preferences can be so different? We obviously don't all agree on everything, so how can we be unified? The answer is seen when our *priorities* are aligned, no matter what our *preferences* are. When our eyes are fixed on the main priorities clearly expressed in the Kingdom of God, we're elevated beyond our worship styles, beyond our political affiliations, beyond our country of origin, and beyond our social status. The right priorities will unify us, even when we disagree.

Priorities clarify the day to day. If you walked into my office today, you'd see two signs. One says "simplify" and the other says "clarify." Both are independently important, but I've learned that you can't have one without the other. It's not very helpful when something is simple, but not clear. For example, I can tell my family that I'd like to go on a vacation. Simple enough, but there are so many additional details that require clarification. Where are we going? When are we going? How will we get there? Who will we see? Where will we stay? The list is endless, and when it comes to simplicity and clarity for Christ followers, the same is true. It's a simple thing to say that we should be living a life of purpose in God's Kingdom, but that's not very clear. Much like taking a vacation with my family, the list of questions becomes endless as we try to discern what that might mean for our day to day. This is exactly where the right priorities come into play. When we have the right priorities, they'll serve to clarify what it really means to live day to day in Christ's Kingdom.

Priorities prevent us from settling for less. The right priorities are standard-setting, yet can often feel beyond us and sometimes hard to live up to. When we experience such feelings, we encounter the temptation to create a narrative in our minds that gives us an excuse to settle for something lesser. Maintaining our focus on the right priorities allows us to regularly redirect and stay on target in life. As we allow God to pull us into His highest priorities, we gain an ever-increasing discernment of what's best, and a courage to view it with fresh eyes. In the following verses, Paul gives voice to such a discernment that is accessible to any person who has experienced The Great Exchange:

> *"And it is my prayer that your love may abound more and more, with knowledge and all discernment, so that you may approve what is excellent, and so be pure and blameless for the day of Christ, filled with the fruit of righteousness that comes through Jesus Christ, to the glory and praise of God."*

Philippians 1:9-11

> When we have the right priorities, they'll serve to clarify what it really means to live day to day in Christ's Kingdom.

Our ability to discern or perceive what is best not only helps us to prioritize what's important, but it also aligns our lives with where Jesus is going, and allows us to see and experience The Increase in the process.

High Places

Lurking underneath all the reasons for having the right priorities is the temptation of living a life of compromise. Compromise happens when we accept a standard for something that's less than God's best.

And it's no small matter.

Compromise represents the greatest pandemic of our day because it threatens the life that is most important to any person following Jesus — the life of He. To be infected with compromise in any form is to invite erosion to begin as it relates to the bedrock of our faith. And not just in our day. Compromise has always been a temptation to those who align with God. Consider a well-known and highly-regarded king in ancient Israel named Uzziah. The people knew the Messiah would eventually come through the line of Judah (which did ultimately happen in Jesus) and every king that assumed the throne would provide a sense of new hope and anticipation for the people ... is this the One? While Uzziah (also known as Azariah) showed great promise in many ways, he ultimately failed before God. His failure came through the cracked-open door of compromise.

"In the twenty-seventh year of Jeroboam king of Israel,
Azariah the son of Amaziah, king of Judah, began to reign.
He was sixteen years old when he began to reign, and he
reigned fifty-two years in Jerusalem. His mother's name was
Jecoliah of Jerusalem. And he did what was right in the eyes
of the Lord, according to all that his father Amaziah had
done. Nevertheless, the high places were not taken away. The
people still sacrificed and made offerings on the high places."

2 Kings 15:1-4

Although Uzziah accomplished a great deal for the good of the people, he failed to destroy the high places, which were the pagan shrines in Judah. A careful reading also reveals that his father (Amaziah) and grandfather (Joash) had also failed to destroy the very same high places. Like father, like son, like grandson.

Every society since then has had its own version of high places, and so has every heart. As nations, cities, and individuals, these places of compromise represent idols that God has expressly commanded us to tear down. But instead of doing so, we often write a different narrative that allows us to keep them alive and well. They're places where intentional and unintentional idol worship is tolerated, even celebrated — where a *god* reigns above *The God*, and Me rules above He. We may live basically good lives and yet miss doing what is most important. A lifetime of doing good is not enough if we make the crucial mistake of not following God with *all* our hearts. A true follower of God won't get it perfect every time, but he or she will ultimately put God first in all areas of life.

For many, the American Dream has become a high place, defined by having the perfect house, the perfect spouse, the perfect job, and the perfect social network. For others, the high places consist of the never-ending pursuit of fame, followers, and influence. And while sex, money, and power are obvious potential high places for all of us, there are also a myriad of *virtuous* causes we can also attach ourselves to that might actually masquerade as a Kingdom priority, but in reality carry the weight of something far less.

> To be infected with compromise in any form is to invite erosion to proceed as it relates to the bedrock of our faith.

Whatever the high place looks like, they all have the same lie attached to them. They promise something that seems like water, but only leaves people with greater thirst than when they first tasted it. High places are the perfect visual for what a competing priority really looks like. In time, those competing priorities become the enemy of the best priorities. We can all be tempted to settle for something *good*, even when God is offering us the very *best*. Staying true to the right priorities will always differentiate the good from the best.

Listen to the final verse of the Book of 1 John. After five chapters imploring his readers to cling to the foundation of faith that is found in Jesus and resist the allure of anything lesser, the Apostle John puts one final exclamation point on his message: "Dear children, keep yourselves from idols" (1 John 5:21). It's often said that a person's final words reveal what they most want you to hear. In this instance, it's as if John is trying to shout this one final six-word warning about the inherent danger of becoming enticed by anything other than Jesus. The risk of our high places is significant. Whatever we elevate to that high place will capture our attention and our affections over time, but the remedy is found as we discover that which is preeminent. We must surrender to the fact there's an ideal hierarchy in our lives, and that God is the one who defines it. There must be an ongoing process of refining what we're fixing our eyes upon. The thoughts and affections of our hearts and minds must be identified, challenged, and when appropriate, destroyed.

CONCLUSION

This may seem difficult, if not impossible. But I assure you, it's possible when our priorities become the very same priorities that Jesus calls us to. We're about to head into a discussion that clarifies a few things. You see, in the end, Christ only has two priorities for us — *for all of us.*

But before we get there, I invite you to pause, take a breath, and absorb the following verses from Colossians. Read both the English Standard Version translation and The Message paraphrase. Both speak powerfully into the priorities that we're all being called to embrace and act upon.

> *"If then you have been raised with Christ, seek the things*
> *that are above, where Christ is, seated at the right hand of*
> *God. Set your minds on things that are above, not on things*
> *that are on earth. For you have died, and your life is hidden*
> *with Christ in God. When Christ who is your life appears,*
> *then you also will appear with him in glory."*

Colossians 3:1-4

(ESV)

"So if you're serious about living this new resurrection life with Christ, act like it. Pursue the things over which Christ presides. Don't shuffle along, eyes to the ground, absorbed with the things right in front of you. Look up, and be alert to what is going on around Christ—that's where the action is. See things from his perspective. Your old life is dead. Your new life, which is your real life—even though invisible to spectators—is with Christ in God. He is your life. When Christ (your real life, remember) shows up again on this earth, you'll show up, too—the real you, the glorious you. Meanwhile, be content with obscurity, like Christ."

Colossians 3:1-4
(The Message)

When we set our hearts on things above, we begin to experience the only high place that actually belongs in our lives. In so doing, we'll become people who pursue the priorities over which Jesus presides. We'll refuse to shuffle along with our eyes staring at the ground, and instead we'll become people who are always looking up, and who are always growing in our understanding of what's happening around Jesus.

So I invite you into a place where you act upon your convictions. I invite you to commit to Jesus in both word and deed, and to learn to walk as He walked.

I invite you into a conversation about priorities.

So when you're ready, turn the page, and let's dive in!

CHAPTER 10

Love God

START HERE

SCAN TO WATCH

Living By *DESIGN* Rather Than Default

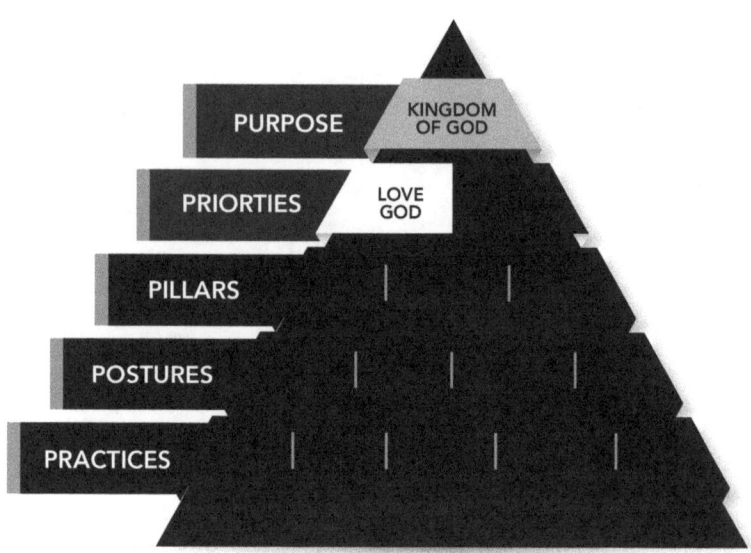

When a team is in a must-score situation at the end of a football game, offenses at every level run a series of plays called a "Two-Minute Drill." This two-minute offensive scheme is a make-or-break, last-minute attempt to put points on the board. Back at Stanford, whenever we ran our version of a two-minute drill under Coach Walsh, every player on the offense intimately knew the six to eight plays he'd call. We also knew that he'd only call those plays. The simplicity of his approach freed us up to not worry about any surprises that would have left us uncertain or flat-footed. When the clock was running down, and the sense of urgency was pressing around us from every side, we knew the prioritized plays Coach Walsh had boiled everything down to. We knew those were the most effective plays, and they were the plays that would put us in the best position to score.

There are so many parallels for us in living a life that embraces the two-minute-drill concept. That being said, there is one that stands above the rest and is worthy of our consideration. As we're learning to live every *Today* for *That Day*, one of the most effective things we can do is to ask what everything in this life boils down to? If our purpose is His Kingdom, and if two main Priorities are what support a life aligned with that purpose, then what would Jesus boil it all down to?

What Must I Do?

In Luke 10, we're introduced to a man with considerable knowledge and influence who's asking the very same question. We don't know much about him but various translations describe him as "an expert in religious law," "an expert in the law," or "a lawyer." Whoever he was, he felt qualified enough to attempt to "put Jesus to the test." On the surface, it appears he's asking Jesus to "boil it all down" for him. However, what initially seems innocent and authentic soon reveals itself to be far less so when we're given a key insight into the condition of his heart. Luke helps us see this man's *true* motivation. As the story unfolds, it becomes clear that his motives were to trap Jesus within a web of religious formulas that he and others like him had created.

> *"And behold, a lawyer stood up to put him to the test, saying, 'Teacher, what shall I do to inherit eternal life?'*
>
> *"He (Jesus) said to him, 'What is written in the Law? How do you read it?'*
>
> *"And he (the lawyer) answered, 'You shall love the Lord your God with all your heart and with all your soul and with all your strength and with all your mind, and your neighbor as yourself.'*
>
> *"And he (Jesus) said to him, 'You have answered correctly; do this, and you will live.'"*

Luke 10:25-28

Jesus' response is simple and straightforward. While the next part of the story will flip the script on the lawyer, we should pause and ponder this exchange before moving on. As we do so, we'll be given the True North provisions we need to live every Today, for That Day.

> Living in response to the love God has already shown us may be the most important paradigm shift we make when it comes to this first and greatest priority of loving God.

OF FIRST IMPORTANCE

When Jesus affirms the aforementioned "test question" from the lawyer, His affirmation gives us a clearer understanding of what it means to truly love God. Jesus' answer connects with His Jewish audience who would have been familiar with the primary importance of loving God and loving one's neighbor. As we'll discover, the four components of heart, soul, mind and strength each point to a nuanced understanding of our nature as people. If we are to love God with our entirety, then what does that look like?

With All Your Heart — Our heart represents our affections. We all know what it's like to have our hearts drawn toward something. That drive within us — those burning affections — must be an ever-increasing movement toward God. This is where the higher places are torn down, and where the preeminence of Christ is proclaimed in our surrender. That warning about higher places echoes in Jesus' teaching in Mark 4 about the thorns and thistles of life that can choke us. He tells us that "the desires for other things" will always be a driving force in missing the mark of our primary purpose

(Mark 4:19). In addition, the writer of Proverbs helps us see what's really at stake when it comes to our hearts: "Keep your heart with all vigilance, for from it flow the springs of life" (Proverbs 4:23).

With All Your Soul — The soul is the relational component of our being, and it's that part of us that's eternal, and cannot be destroyed with the death of our bodies (Matthew 10:28). It's the most real version of us, so the stakes couldn't be higher. Our souls are absolutely sacred, and represent the deepest part of what makes us human. When we love God with all our soul, we're leaning into Him with the most authentic and true version of us, then allowing any protective walls we've built to come crashing down before Him.

With All Your Strength — Our strength represents our fortitude. It involves our will, and is also commonly paired in Scripture with our courage. In this case, the type of strength being referred to has nothing to do with the strength of our bodies. Even though we'll all experience diminishing physical wellness as we get older, that reality doesn't constrict or restrain us from loving God with all our strength. Much like the Lord told Joshua, we're all told to be strong and courageous in every step of the journey He's mapped out for us (Joshua 1:9).

With All Your Mind — The mind represents the center of all thought. It's the storehouse for our frame of reference. It's where paradigms and frameworks for all things reside. To love God with all our minds means that the way we perceive life becomes increasingly inspired by the way God created it in the first place. As Paul reminds the believers in Rome (and to us today), a mind that's being renewed day by day unlocks much of the transformation we'll experience as we walk with Jesus:

"Do not conform to the pattern of this world,
but be transformed by the renewing of your mind. Then
you will be able to test and approve what God's will is—
his good, pleasing and perfect will."

Romans 12:2

(NIV)

At the end of the day, loving God is possessing a deep hunger for what He wants most. It's a passionate caring for what He cares about. It's something we must get right, or risk falling into a performance-based version of Christianity, rather than the grace-based life that's offered to us in Christ ... that we receive with the Great Exchange.

> It's a proclamation of allegiance toward God,
> declaring that the highest place is held by only One.

OUR RESPONSE

Living in response to the love God has already shown us may be the most important paradigm shift we make when it comes to this first and greatest priority of loving God. We've likely heard countless sermons that implore us to love God more. But if we are the ones being asked to initiate that love — to feel a certain feeling, or to force a certain emotion into existence — then we'll experience something far less than what God intends. We'll also experience the guilt of not being able to do it. Have you ever had someone tell you to feel more of a certain thing? Statements like, "You shouldn't feel that way," or "You need to feel more _____," just don't work. We don't have that kind of capacity on our own.

In 1 John 4:7-21, John launches into a lengthy discourse about love. He talks about God's love for us, our love for Him, and our love for one another. It's beautiful, breathtaking, and a poignant reminder of what's really true. Toward the end of the discourse, John drops a phrase that informs the way we love God and others.

"We love because he first loved us."

1 John 4:19

In magnitude, God's love is higher, wider, and deeper than our love will ever be. In the created order, it's His intimate love that landed on us long before we could beat Him to the punch. Love for God is sourced in Him, not in us. We *respond* rather than *initiate*.

With this hallowed truth at the forefront, we really need to be honest with ourselves. If the very essence of God's character is love (1 John 4:8), and if we're not experiencing moments of childlike wonder in the unspeakable glory of that love, then it's important to ask ourselves why. Have we traded the intimacy of *knowing* God for an academic understanding of *knowing about* Him? Have the hardships and struggles of life caused us to adopt a posture of uncertainty when it comes to His love for us? Or perhaps we've been hurt by leaders who claim to represent God, and so it's become nearly impossible for us to reconcile their failures with the loving God they claim to represent. Or maybe, we're just plain exhausted with try-harder Christianity, and on the verge of not believing anymore.

Whatever the case, responding to the revealed love of God as written about in Scripture is the answer. God's love is always the answer, even when we can't find the vocabulary to ask the questions. It's written all throughout the Bible. Let these following verses not just inform you, but also pour over you:

"In this the love of God was made manifest among us, that God sent his only Son into the world, so that we might live through him. In this is love, not that we have loved God but that he loved us and sent his Son to be the propitiation for our sins."

1 John 4:9-10

"See what kind of love the Father has given to us, that we should be called children of God; and so we are. The reason why the world does not know us is that it did not know him."

1 John 3:1

"But God shows his love for us in that while we were still sinners, Christ died for us."

Romans 5:8

"For I am sure that neither death nor life, nor angels nor rulers, nor things present nor things to come, nor powers, nor height nor depth, nor anything else in all creation, will be able to separate us from the love of God in Christ Jesus our Lord."

Romans 8:38-39

There is no end to the love of God. It doesn't come and go, based on how He feels about our actions. It's continually lavished upon us because we are His children. It covers us, protects us, fights for us, and chases after us.

This is the very love we crave. This is the very relationship our hearts cry out for. When we begin to live with this sense of wide-eyed discovery, we grow increasingly aware of being the imperfect recipients of a love that has no limits. Day in and day out, our loving response back to God's love for us *has* to be the single greatest priority of our lives.

LOVE AND OBEDIENCE

Scripture often discusses the intricate relationship between loving God and obeying God. It's often misunderstood, and warrants an important discourse here. If we're being honest, most of us hear the word "obedience" and often want to run in the opposite direction. While it's true that our obedience doesn't ever *earn* the love of God, our obedience does however serve as evidence *of* our love for Him. Our obedience is simply another way to respond to His great love for us.

> *"Jesus answered him, 'If anyone loves me, he will keep my word, and my Father will love him, and we will come to him and make our home with him. Whoever does not love me does not keep my words. And the word that you hear is not mine but the Father's who sent me.'"*

John 14:23-24

When most of us read this, we tend to be drawn into the commands we don't keep, the rules we don't follow, and the teachings of Jesus we don't obey.

While those are all realities that shouldn't be overlooked, they must never become our focus when it comes to matters of obedience. Staying faithful to the teachings of Jesus is far more about who we serve and where our allegiance in life is sourced, and far less about where we get it wrong. We must resist the lure of some safe and predictable formula, all the while missing out on a vision of the magnificent and untamed glory of God.

At a practical level, when we walk where Jesus is already walking, we're obeying God.

When we live our lives *Today* with *That Day* in mind, we're obeying God.

When we fix our eyes on Jesus standing at the finish line, we're obeying God.

When we say yes to Jesus in any way, we're obeying God.

We're drawing a line in the sand when we do these things. We're joining together with the bold proclamation that Joshua declared:

> *"Now therefore fear the Lord and serve him in sincerity*
> *and in faithfulness. Put away the gods that your fathers*
> *served beyond the River and in Egypt, and serve the Lord.*
> *And if it is evil in your eyes to serve the Lord, choose this*
> *day whom you will serve, whether the gods your fathers*
> *served in the region beyond the River, or the gods of the*
> *Amorites in whose land you dwell. But as for me and*
> *my house, we will serve the Lord."*

Joshua 24:14-15

This is love and obedience. This is the choice you make for yourself, and for your family. This is the clear and visible line in the sand. It's a proclamation of allegiance toward God, declaring that the highest place is held by only One. It's an acknowledgment of His presence everywhere, and a wholehearted response to His love without limitation.

CONCLUSION

The first and foremost priority is to love God with everything we are and everything we have. It's simple, but not easy. It's clear, but with nuances. It's direct, but not formulaic.

And it's also unfinished.

The story in Luke 10 doesn't end with only one priority. Jesus pushes us all into a second priority.

And that's exactly where the journey takes us next.

CHAPTER 11

Love Others

105

START HERE

SCAN TO WATCH

Living By *DESIGN* Rather Than Default

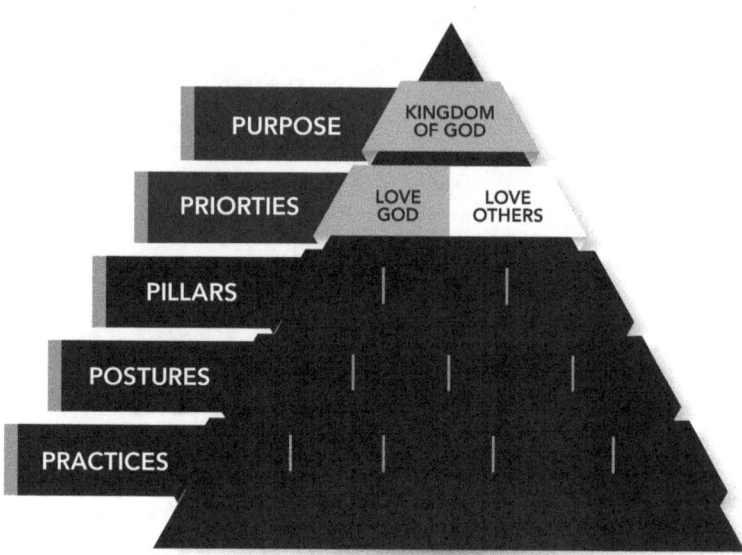

In Chapter 10 we looked at the story involving Jesus and the lawyer, and discovered that the first priority of a life in Christ's Kingdom is a deep and abiding love for God. We learned that this love is both multifaceted and is a response to the love He first showed us, not the other way around. In addition, we know that this love is demonstrated in our willingness to place Him above any other high places in our lives we've chosen to exalt.

The account in Luke 10 continues, and the encounter between Jesus and the expert in the law is far from over. While our first priority of loving God is more than evident, there's a clearly-stated second priority that's equally essential to our understanding of life in God's Kingdom.

For many people, it's often more challenging than the first.

An Ancient and Urgent Dialogue

The second priority is discovered in a conversation within the conversation. The lawyer begins by quoting what he already knows to be true, followed by a response from Jesus.

"And he (the lawyer) answered, 'You shall love the Lord your God with all your heart and with all your soul and with all your strength and with all your mind, and your neighbor as yourself.'

"And he (Jesus) said to him, "You have answered correctly; do this, and you will live."'

Luke 10:27-28

Love God, love others. It is a beautifully succinct distillation of what matters to God. Seems straightforward enough, but the lawyer doesn't leave it there. He's looking for something more — something that feels like justification.

"But he (the lawyer), desiring to justify himself, said to Jesus, 'And who is my neighbor?"'

Luke 10:29

If there was ever the perfect commentary that nails the center of another person's intentions, Luke's phrasing here is spot on: "Desiring to justify himself." While we assume he's asking about justifying himself before God, he may have also been trying to justify himself before those around him. Isn't that how we all approach God and others at some level? We want to do something, say something, pray something, or be something that proves we're okay. There's nothing that shifts our focus away from He and onto Me quite like justifying ourselves for our actions or beliefs. Fortunately for us, whether with the religious elite or the common person, Jesus doesn't play into it. Rather than appeal to a principle, edict, or demand as His answer, Jesus does what He most often does.

He tells a story.

WHO IS MY NEIGHBOR?

You've heard the story, likely countless times. Through the ages, the title we've given it is "The Good Samaritan," but it involves far more than this central character.

> *"Jesus replied, 'A man was going down from Jerusalem to Jericho, and he fell among robbers, who stripped him and beat him and departed, leaving him half dead. Now by chance a priest was going down that road, and when he saw him he passed by on the other side. So likewise a Levite, when he came to the place and saw him, passed by on the other side. But a Samaritan, as he journeyed, came to where he was, and when he saw him, he had compassion. He went to him and bound up his wounds, pouring on oil and wine. Then he set him on his own animal and brought him to an inn and took care of him. And the next day he took out two denarii and gave them to the innkeeper, saying, "Take care of him, and whatever more you spend, I will repay you when I come back." Which of these three, do you think, proved to be a neighbor to the man who fell among the robbers?'*
>
> *He (the lawyer) said, 'The one who showed him mercy.'*
>
> *And Jesus said to him, 'You go, and do likewise.'"*
>
> Luke 10:30-37

As the expert in religious law listened to this story, he would have embraced the Priest and the Levite as the people in his tribe. He would have connected those two with an ability to bring the proper resources into an emergency situation like this. If the story ended with the Priest and Levite passing the injured man by, it would have certainly caused a deep and disruptive stir in the lawyer's heart, and would have given him pause to consider the story as he walked away from the scene. But Jesus keeps going.

> Loving our neighbor will often feel messy and scary, compounded by the doubting voice that asks us if we're really willing to inconvenience ourselves and enter into the situation.

As Jesus continues the story, and as the lawyer continues to listen, we're introduced to the central figure in the exchange — a Samaritan. Historically speaking, Samaritans were despised by devout Jews. For this reason, a Samaritan becoming the hero of the story would have been seen as a mistake, at best, in the mind of the lawyer, and heresy at worst.

Knowing this, as Jesus begins to wind the story to its surprise ending, He directs His gaze toward the expert in the law and asks him a question that will reveal the condition of his heart: "Which of these three, do you think, proved to be a neighbor to the man who fell among the robbers?" What began with the lawyer putting Jesus to the test concludes with Jesus leading the witness by asking the most significant question yet. The expert in the law replied, "The one who showed him mercy." He's right, of course, and then the conclusion comes. It's a directive the lawyer didn't want to hear.

"And Jesus said to him, 'You go, and do likewise.'"

Luke 10:37

And there it is. Go and do, just like the Samaritan did. Loving God and loving people will always involve *doing* something — not to earn eternal life, but as a Spirit-led byproduct of following the One who gives it. In this story, Jesus refines our understanding of who our neighbor really is.

Our neighbor is our actual neighbor. He might be the elderly widower living next door who lost his wife to cancer the previous year. Our neighbor might be the young family across the street, the struggling single mom working two jobs, or the teenager who feeds his younger siblings breakfast every morning long before he gets them to their school on time. Walk out your front door tonight. As you stand there, look left, then forward, then right. Stand in your backyard and look over your back property line. The homes, the apartment units, or any dwellings that appear within your eyesight are your neighbors.

Our neighbor is anyone we come in contact with, and who might be in need of our help. In the story of the Good Samaritan, this is certainly the case. It helps us expand and redefine our understanding of the people Jesus is telling us to love. These are the people we encounter who need warmth when they're cold, encouragement when they're uncertain, or relief when they're suffering.

Whether they're our physical neighbor or other people we come in contact with, loving our neighbor should be a daily occurrence. It happens as we're in the middle of our events, our errands, and our job commitments. It's seen in the opportunities we're granted at the grocery store, the ball game, the street corner, and the coffee shop. It involves preparing ourselves for the spontaneity of whoever God places in our path as our lives pull us naturally into those spaces, and beckons us to respond with love and concern. It's the same mindset the Samaritan must have had when he saw the man fighting for his life on the side of the road, and it's the very same mindset that followers of Jesus must have too.

But oftentimes we don't.

> At the very heart of loving others is the abiding hope that, in some miraculous way, people will be directed back to God.

WHAT ARE MY EXCUSES?

Just like the lawyer, when it comes to identifying and showing love to our neighbors, we all have a tendency to justify our inactivity and inaction toward them. We want God and others to think that, even though we *intend* to love others, there are some good and defensible reasons we're not currently engaging as we should.

The Bystander Effect — This term refers to the social psychological phenomenon in which the greater the number of people present, the less likely they are to help a person in distress. Studies have shown that if a person is in a large crowd, it makes them feel less responsible for taking the proper action in an emergency. People either believe someone else will take care of the crisis, or because no one is taking care of it, it's probably not a legitimate emergency in the first place.

Loving Others Can Feel Messy and Scary — We can "what if?" ourselves into a frenzy as we debate whether or not to engage those who appear in need of help. There's also a legitimate fear of what might happen if we choose to stop and enter into another person's duress. Or maybe we're concerned that God might send us to a part of the world that's uncomfortable for us to even consider. Loving our neighbor will often feel messy and scary, compounded by the doubting voice that asks us if we're really willing to inconvenience ourselves and enter into the situation.

HOW SHOULD WE LOVE OTHERS?

If a pivotal part of living a prioritized life is to love others, and if the rubber meets the road in a redefining of who our neighbor really is, then we need a framework for making decisions in real time, in real life. How do we know both when and how to engage and help?

Being Over Doing — Any work of loving others begins with who we are, not what we do. It begins with a relationship of intimacy with Jesus, and then follows where He leads. We're listening to His promptings and impressions, as sheep who recognize the voice of the Shepherd (John 10:27). If we don't think we have what it takes, our confidence is that Jesus already has what it takes, and then some. We're only vessels, after all.

Preparation Over Planning — As we move throughout the commitments and complexities of our days, we should be prepared to turn, pivot, start, and stop. It's far less about planning outcomes, and more about being fully present in the moment that Jesus is offering. He'll create the best desired outcomes, and asks us to be His hands and feet to get there. Loving others is an immediate, bloom-where-you're-planted mindset that any follower of Jesus can and should adopt now, without worrying about outcomes and possibilities.

Authenticity Over Copying — The actions we take in loving others must be authentic to who we are. While I'm inspired by what I see other people doing, that doesn't mean that I should copy them step for step. Just like the story of the loaves and the fish (John 6:1-14), we're being invited by Jesus to bring Him whatever we have, to let that be enough, and to let Him multiply it however He chooses.

Availability Over Ability — Even if we don't have the expertise to solve a situation for a neighbor, there's a beautiful love that's expressed in simply saying, "How can I help?" or "We can figure this thing out together." As we love God completely and find ourselves transformed into what He intends, it will be Jesus loving people through us, bringing His infinite abilities into the moment, and allowing us to experience the Increase of His life in our open-handed responses.

LET YOUR LIGHT SHINE

Lori and I have been blessed to raise four children. We recently drove to California to drop off our youngest daughter, Ashley, at college. Parents who have made this journey already know the deep emotion that promises to unleash itself during those few days. We helped her move into her new living space, made sure all the required documents were in order, and prepared to drive away. As we began to say our goodbyes, my heart was heavy with the weight of the moment. I pulled Ashley aside, looked into her eyes, and said...

"Ashley, I dropped you off at school your whole life, and every time you got out of the car or walked into a classroom, I told you to go and be a light. And in this milestone moment, there's nothing better than for me to tell you the very same thing. So Ashley, go be a light."

It was an emotional drive home for us, but as the minutes turned into hours, Jesus began to remind me of the things He taught His disciples in Matthew 5:

"You are the light of the world. A city set on a hill cannot be hidden. Nor do people light a lamp and put it under a basket, but on a stand, and it gives light to all in the house. In the same way, let your light shine before others, so that they may see your good works and give glory to your Father who is in heaven."

Matthew 5:14-16

At the very heart of loving others is the abiding hope that, in some miraculous way, people will be directed back to God. Addressing a group of people who didn't look or act like the light of the world, Jesus flips the script and calls them exactly that. Have you ever thought about yourself like this? Jesus knows full well that the light we display through our good deeds will glorify the Father in heaven. At the heart of The 3:30 Life is a belief that God has placed us all in unique moments, at unique times, in unique places, with unique designs — all so that we can show others His love without restraint, fear, or overthinking it.

"A new commandment I give to you, that you love one another: just as I have loved you, you also are to love one another. By this all people will know that you are my disciples, if you have love for one another."

John 13:34-35

May we all have the courage to move past our fears. May we have the honesty to move past our excuses, and may we have the vision to move past our yesterdays. You are the light of the world. Today is a new day.

And the moment is now.

CHAPTER 12

Pillars

START HERE

SCAN TO WATCH

Living By *DESIGN* Rather Than Default

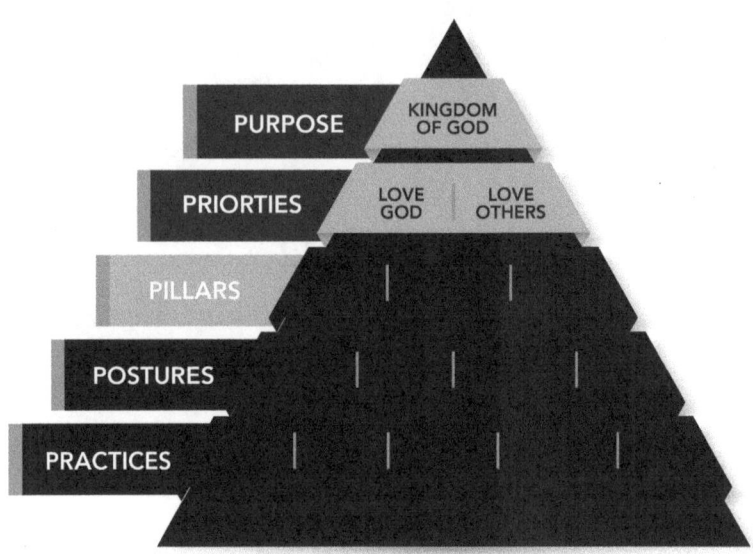

As we've traveled the journey of The 3:30 Life so far, we've already come a long way. We've discovered how John the Baptist's story inspires our own stories. We've talked about the importance of living by design, rather than default. We've explored the truth about who the King *really* is, how we can *really* know Him, and what *really* matters most to Him. We've talked about a singular Kingdom purpose best pursued in our unique running lanes, and we've identified two priorities that arise from Christ's conversation with the expert in religious law, both of which clarify life in His Kingdom.

We've come a long way, but we're not finished yet. There remains a detailed discovery in front of us — one that invites us to move from beyond a place of theory and intellectual head-nodding, and into a lifestyle of proactive and passionate following. For that to ever take place in our lives, we'll need Kingdom support structures to get us to the finish line.

In the previous chapter, we discussed the conversation Jesus had with the lawyer. Those principles should sit with us for the remainder of our days, and that's because *every* Christ follower needs to learn how to best replicate a life of loving God and loving others. We all need to learn how to apply those timeless axioms that help move us from Me to He, and into lives that overflow with a love for our Creator, and a love for the people He created. We need something that's both powerful and actionable, and serves to keep us from drifting into something far less.

We've been talking the talk thus far, but this is where walking the walk begins. This is where the rubber will meet the road, I promise. If we don't figure this out, we'll never experience the increase of Christ's life through ours. We'll bury our Kingdom potential beneath our idols and high places, and choose our personal comfort over God's unique design for our lives.

But it doesn't have to be that way. We can choose something better, something greater, and something higher. We can choose to allow three transformational support structures to hold us, guide us, and keep us from falling.

They're called Pillars.

What Are Pillars?

What image comes to your mind when you hear the word "pillar"? A pillar at the Colosseum in ancient Rome? A steel structure that supports a bridge? Those large wood beams you see when you drive by a construction site? Or maybe you're metaphorically reminded of a key leader in a certain school, community, or church organization?

Webster defines a pillar as "a person or thing regarded as reliable to provide essential support for something larger."

Pillars are reliable and essential. They're supportive and masterfully constructed to be strong and trustworthy. Pillars are understood to be dependable and immoveable as they uphold everything else and prevent collapse.

Pillars support something larger. They're not created for themselves, but for something else. We rarely see a pillar standing on its own. That's because they're created to uphold something greater, larger, and more important. Pillars also serve to further illuminate why the thing being supported is indeed the greater thing.

> We all need to learn how to apply those timeless axioms that help move us from Me to He, and into lives that overflow with a love for our Creator, and a love for the people He created.

WHY DO WE NEED PILLARS?

As we follow Jesus, pillars may be the structures we need the most and recognize the least. They help take the lofty and ethereal matters of faith, and make them tangible. They help us think rightly about the Two Priorities of loving God and loving people. Pillars help us conceive of the right notions and ideas, giving us a framework for thinking. They're what God Himself builds our lives upon, and they shape the perspective through which we see the world around us. Thankfully, we serve a God who wants His Kingdom to flourish in the lives of everyone, and He's anxious to give us the paradigm shift we need for that to happen on earth, just like it is in heaven.

This is precisely where the Pillars come into play.

Pillars anchor us. They provide a firm hold within the bedrock of the Kingdom — that realm where God is the one and only King. If our hope and prayer is to live our lives every day in light of That Day, then these Pillars will support and enable that life, consistently placing it before us. We become anchored to an eternal understanding of who God is, and they help us see who we really are.

Pillars guide us. In addition to providing anchors in our lives, the right pillars also provide guardrails for us to live by. By definition, a guardrail protects and maintains a pathway that has boundaries all along the way, given to us for directional clarity. Pillars guide us and help us follow Jesus along the narrow road of true and abundant Life.

THE THREE PILLARS

The Kingdom of Heaven has come, and it's begging to be manifested and proclaimed in the real, everyday lives of people like you and me. In my own personal experience, the following three Pillars have become the most real and authentic expressions of The 3:30 Life, and invite me into loving God and people better than I did yesterday.

Pillar #1: We are in Christ.

Pillar #2: We are Partners.

Pillar #3: We are on Mission.

Simply stated, we are people who are in Christ, as partners, on mission.

The Three Pillars will anchor us, guiding us along a way that seems narrow, but that leads to abundant life. They'll support an ever-increasing proclamation of God's Kingdom in us, and through us. They'll push us, prod us, and provoke us. Best of all, they'll help us proclaim the Name that is above every name with clarity into our world.

> They help take the lofty and ethereal matters of faith, and make them tangible.

It bears repeating: We've come a long way, but we're not home yet. There remains a detailed discovery that still awaits us — one that invites us to move from theory to practice, and from intellectual ascent to passionate following.

So buckle up.

Hold on.

And dive in.

Because these three Pillars will change everything.

CHAPTER 13

In Christ

START HERE

SCAN TO WATCH

Living By *DESIGN* Rather Than Default

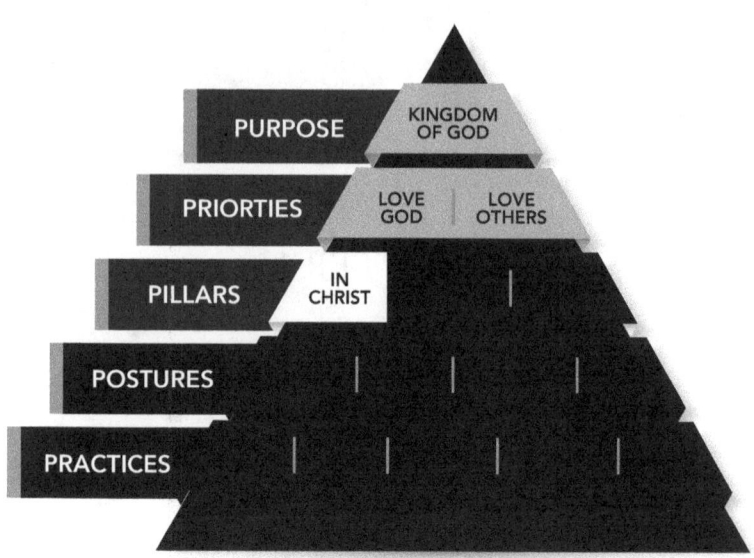

We all encounter many new people in the regular rhythms of life. Whether it's during our social gatherings, at our kids' athletic games, in our work environments, or at the variety of events we attend, new conversations with people we've never met before inevitably happen. When these encounters begin, it's likely the conversation will eventually get to the question, "So ... what do you *do*?" Our answers obviously come in various forms, but almost always boil down to the jobs we have and the things we do during our waking hours.

I'm a landscaper.

I'm a teacher.

I'm a volunteer.

I'm a graphic designer.

I'm a student.

I'm a parent.

I'm retired, but I used to be a doctor.

I'm an accountant.

The list goes on and on. When we use these labels in our conversations, we're helping other people identify how we spend our time, and what skills we've picked up along the way. Obviously, there's nothing inherently wrong or harmful about the labels we give ourselves. But things can quickly go south when we allow those labels to define us, and when we start to derive our value from them. Worse yet, when others are allowed to equate these labels about what we do with who we are, it often prompts them to categorize us — sifting us into their own hierarchies of importance.

The issue here is identity, and as you'll soon discover, there's more at stake than meets the eye. Identity is not only at the core of the first Pillar that supports the The 3:30 Life journey, but it's the fundamental reality we must get right. Above and beyond whatever labels we use to describe what we do, as followers of Jesus the most transforming and foundational understanding of our core identity is discovered in two simple words.

In Christ.

Beyond jobs and labels and skills and earnings, our foremost identity is that we are designed to be *in Christ*. And that, friends, is something we must know, something we must never forget, and something we must lean into every day.

KNOW YOU'RE IN CHRIST

It's impossible to read the New Testament writers without encountering the phrase "in Christ" at almost every turn. The words from the mouth of Jesus are the cornerstone of our identity, and are discovered when Jesus uses "in me" as He preaches and teaches. The phrase "in Christ" occurs over 160 times across Paul's 13 letters alone.

"Therefore, if anyone is in Christ, he is a new creation. The old has passed away; behold, the new has come."

2 Corinthians 5:17

"There is therefore now no condemnation for those who are in Christ Jesus."

Romans 8:1

"For we are his workmanship, created in Christ Jesus for good works, which God prepared beforehand, that we should walk in them."

Ephesians 2:10

Beyond jobs and labels and skills and earnings, our foremost identity is that we are designed to be *in Christ*.

For a person to be in Christ, there is an assumption of rebirth — that new starting point I've called The Great Exchange (discussed in Chapter 4). It describes that moment in time when we recognize and respond to the amazing offer from God to be saved from our sins and to receive His free gift of eternal life by placing our faith and trust in Jesus. The ultimate identity swap happens as Jesus pays the price for what we deserve and we receive His very life in return. In The Great Exchange, the life of Jesus is given *to* us, to live *in* us, and to be seen *through* us.

At a football game, there are thousands of people in the stands who wear the players' jerseys, but who aren't actually on the team. We call those people fans. In this world, there are many fans of Jesus who aren't followers. For those who have put their faith in Jesus, the result is that they've been restored back into the family of God — a family where God is our Father, and where we are sons and daughters of the King!

"For you did not receive the spirit of slavery to fall back into fear, but you have received the Spirit of adoption as sons, by whom we cry, 'Abba! Father!'"

Romans 8:15

That being said, as true as this is, I believe one of the best ways to understand our identity "in Christ" is from one of the most popular parables Jesus ever told. It's found in Luke 15, and it's called "The Prodigal Son." More than likely, you've heard it before.

The parable begins with a discontented and frustrated son disrespecting his father by asking for his inheritance early (a custom usually reserved for after a father's death). His father agrees, grants his son's request, and watches as his boy walks away. The son proceeds to waste all of his money on "reckless living." He reaches the very bottom of the barrel when his money has been squandered and his riches depleted. At that point, just to survive from one day to the next, the son takes a job working on a pig farm. Unable to afford even a simple meal, he craves the food the pigs are eating.

After a long while, the son wakes up one morning, takes an honest look at his circumstances and makes the courageous decision to return home. For anyone who's ever hit rock bottom, it's easy to see that a return to the father is the best and only solution here. The son crafts a plan to be taken back in by his father. His offer will be to work as a hired hand in his father's home, because his actions have disqualified him from returning to the actual family. The son even rehearses exactly what he'll say when he sees his father. With his plan in place, he begins the long journey home.

But what he expects to happen next isn't what he experiences. It's something better. Something *far* better.

As the son turns from the main road onto the walkway leading up to his house, he lifts his eyes upward, off of his dirt-caked sandals, and up toward the last thing he ever expected to see. His father is throwing off his robe, and is now sprinting unencumbered toward him with arms open wide.

> *"But while he was still a long way off, his father saw him and felt compassion, and ran and embraced him and kissed him."*

Luke 15:20

In the emotion of the moment, the son launches into his speech — the one about becoming a hired hand — but the father isn't even listening. The son confesses his sin against the father, and then says, "I am not worthy to be called your son." But the father, filled with compassion and love, responds in a manner consistent with his character.

He throws a party.

It's a welcome-home party. It's a party that celebrates the joy he feels at his youngest son's homecoming. The only statements of judgment and accusation come not from the father, but from the older brother. At that point there is a direct conversation between the father and his oldest son, and then the story simply ends.

It's almost as if Jesus leaves the story open-ended so that generations to follow could take the story, and explore hundreds of different possible discoveries and applications. But I only have one question. Just one.

At any point in this story did the actions of the son stop him from being a son?

The answer is obvious. The son was always a son. He never quit being a son. His birth determined his identity. It's not because of his faithfulness or faithlessness, but because of the love of his father.

You want to know what it means to be in Christ? It means *that*. It means *exactly that*. It means that we are sons and daughters of the Father. It means that our faithfulness or faithlessness can never qualify or disqualify our adoption into God's family.

It means that we are home.

Whether you find yourself pursuing God's Kingdom at every turn, eating with the pigs and ashamed to go home, or somewhere in between, if you've experienced The Great Exchange and gone from death to life, then your identity is secure. You are in Christ, and no person or situation will *ever* take that away.

Don't Forget You're In Christ

As we learn to embrace the weight of its truth, our identity in Christ is nothing less than astounding. There's a newfound security that pushes us past our insecurities, and a certainty that triumphs over our fears.

As fallible humans, we'll always be prone to forget our new identity. Add to that the reality of a defense on the field that's working overtime to make us doubt and question that identity, and it's easy to see how we might forget who we really are, and Whose we really are.

In the case of the prodigal son, his moment of remembering happens when "he comes to his senses," and he decides to go back home. Even though he thinks he's disqualified himself as a true son, his father knows the truth, and reminds him of his true identity. While he'll remember that day as long as he lives, he'll need constant reminders of the ongoing truth it holds.

We're all like that, at least to some degree. We often forget the most important things. Whenever I sign my name, I almost always sign it "In Christ." For years, people have commented on what a great testimony that is to people. I always appreciate the encouragement, and I pray that it's true. But honestly, I don't sign those words for the sake of other people. I sign those words so that I'm regularly reminded of Whose I really am.

We must remember that at all times, but if remembering our identity in Christ is one side of the coin, the other side is called *abiding*.

I needed to learn that our doing is always sourced in
our being, and our being is always sourced "in Christ."

ABIDE IN CHRIST

The word "abide" isn't one we hear too often, but it captures a very important part of this first Pillar. When we abide in Christ, we lean into Him. We position ourselves as near to Him as possible, no matter what the circumstances of our lives are.

Jesus illustrated this truth for us in a well-known passage about vines, branches, fruit, and a Gardener.

> *"I am the true vine, and my Father is the vinedresser. Every branch in me that does not bear fruit he takes away, and every branch that does bear fruit he prunes, that it may bear more fruit. Already you are clean because of the word that I have spoken to you. Abide in me, and I in you. As the branch cannot bear fruit by itself, unless it abides in the vine, neither can you, unless you abide in me. I am the vine; you are the branches. Whoever abides in me and I in him, he it is that bears much fruit, for apart from me you can do nothing. If anyone does not abide in me he is thrown away like a branch and withers; and the branches are gathered, thrown into the fire, and burned."*

John 15:1-6

For those who are in Christ, abiding in Him isn't an option to consider at a later date, nor is it another task on our to-do list. Look at the father in the story Jesus told. Who wouldn't want to lean into that kind of love? Who wouldn't want to abide in that kind of home?

Abiding is the natural response for those who are in Christ. It's also where any good fruit comes from. When Jesus says "apart from me you can do nothing," He means that literally. Jesus tells His followers that abiding in Him is the only way to live our lives every day, with an acute awareness of That Day. He never commands us to "produce" anything. Instead, we're the ones who "bear" the fruit that He produces. Fruit is the natural byproduct of being properly connected to the vine.

Abiding puts Jesus on display in our lives to a watching world. Abiding activates a life of He not Me. When we're aligned with Him, it's His life that people are interacting with, through us. Those moments are filled with the fruit He desires, and will become the very Increase of Christ.

> There's a newfound security that pushes us past our insecurities, and a certainty that triumphs over our fears.

CONCLUSION

So think back to those labels we began with: Landscaper, doctor, accountant, and others. Now, ask yourself, "What's my label?" Stop for a minute, and think about your answer. Do you start with the things you do, or with the reality of Whose you are?

This may be hard to imagine, but there will be a day when your label won't be true anymore. We'll transition into another job, we'll retire, or we'll completely reinvent our days. But dear friends ... there will never be a day when Christ followers are not found to be "in Christ."

There will never be a day when your true identity is not...

Son. Daughter.

Please don't rush past this. Personally, when I finally understood this — when my only true identity finally sunk in — it changed everything. It has always been true, but I needed to recognize and embrace it. I needed to learn that our doing is always sourced in our being, and our being is always sourced "in Christ."

We are in His family.

We belong to Him.

We are His sons and daughters.

We must abide in that reality.

CHAPTER 14

As Partners

START HERE

SCAN TO WATCH

Living By *DESIGN* Rather Than Default

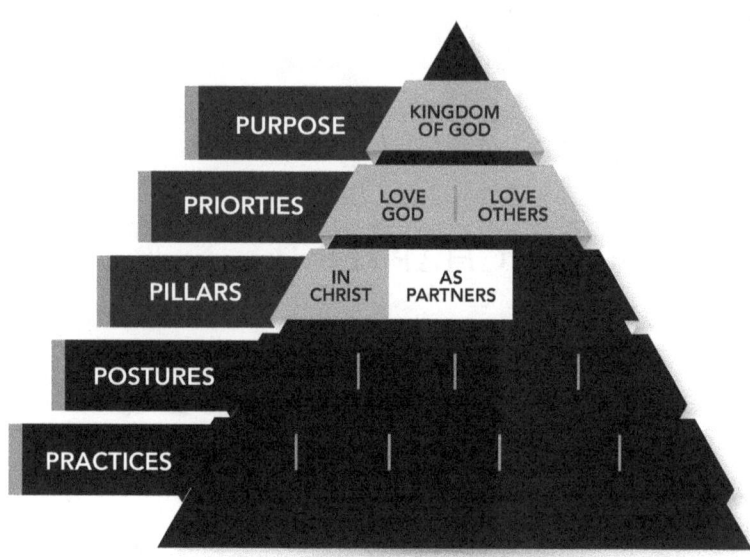

It's easy for us to judge the success of any great team by the skill of their players. We all assume that when a team is full of high-profile athletes, who are the best at their craft, then that team is more likely to win the championship. However, the skill of the players is only one part of a winning equation. We've all seen an uber-talented collection of players lose, and conversely, we've also witnessed a team of less-skilled players hoist the prize at the end. Why is that?

One primary reason is because great teams are most often made up of great teammates. Does skill matter? Of course it does. But if every person on the team isn't continually becoming the very best teammate they can be, then the likelihood of winning decreases. The greatest teams are the ones who've learned to become the most cohesive unit possible, even if they don't have the most talented players. The whole becomes greater than the sum of its parts, and the greatest teams are always an extension of something much larger than themselves. While it's true that professional sports teams include trainers and executives and people who fulfill a myriad of other roles, there's a special interconnectivity between the *coaches* and the *players* that becomes a consistent predictor of success.

Through the years in my conversations with Coach Walsh, the discussions often focused on the importance of becoming great teammates as part of a collective whole. On one particular occasion he said, "We're all connected as a unit and that includes the coaches and the players. We're all using the same language, and it's all related." Coach went on to say, "Your interaction with other people is absolutely critical, from the standpoint of your ability to communicate and express yourself and listen. I think one of the values we had was we just had an atmosphere that nurtured and developed; an atmosphere where people had confidence in each other, believed in each other, and responded to each other." As I listened to Coach Walsh say these things, I couldn't help seeing the spiritual parallel, especially as it relates to living in the family of God.

The 3:30 Life assumes that each of us is continually growing and pursuing the unique race we're given to run. It pushes us to live by God's design, not by our own whims and desires. This life flourishes as we embrace one another, all the while admitting our desperate need for each other. We are *partners*, and we are *together*.

Partnership is the second Pillar of The 3:30 Life. It will anchor us to the reality of becoming the best teammates possible. We are designed to live in Christ, as partners.

As Partners With Each Other

An integral part of The 3:30 Life will *always* involve other people. One definition of a partnership is "when two or more people work together to complete a task." We can't get around the biblical mandate of partnership, especially when viewed in light of what Scripture says about it. The phrase "one another" leaps off the pages of the New Testament, occurring over 100 times. The New Testament believers understood the importance of living in community with others, and they intentionally discovered how to best do that. Life spent together is essential for followers of Jesus. We can't grow, flourish, or truly follow Him without others.

> When we're brought into the family of God, our uniqueness grows as we give ourselves away to others around us.

But that's not all. In addition to the fact that we need others, we're also faced with the unmistakable truth that others need us. The Apostle Paul writes:

> *"For as in one body we have many members, and*
> *the members do not all have the same function, so we,*
> *though many, are one body in Christ, and*
> *individually members one of another."*

Romans 12:4-5

Though we all share one purpose, we each have a unique role to fulfill. The Spirit of God gives us eyes to see the opportunities that are meant for us, serving God's plans and purposes wherever He's placed us. When we're brought into the family of God, our uniqueness grows as we give ourselves away to others around us. We complement each other, while at the same time we surrender our pursuits to the collective whole. When this happens in real time, Jesus is clearly represented to a watching world.

At the most basic level, we're fundamentally learning to love each other. In the previous chapter, we looked at the fruit of a life lived "in Christ," and the very next thing John talks about in that same passage is love.

> *"This is my commandment, that you love one another as I have loved you. Greater love has no one than this, that someone lay down his life for his friends. You are my friends if you do what I command you. No longer do I call you servants, for the servant does not know what his master is doing; but I have called you friends, for all that I have heard from my Father I have made known to you. You did not choose me, but I chose you and appointed you that you should go and bear fruit and that your fruit should abide, so that whatever you ask the Father in my name, he may give it to you. These things I command you, so that you will love one another."*

John 15:12-17

We can't possibly miss the fact that the fruit of The 3:30 Life will always, always, always be expressed in the way we love. This love, especially within the Body of Christ, isn't based on how we feel. If love is a command, then our feelings are a terrible gauge for understanding the essence of what it really is. We are partners both with Jesus as the Head of the body and with one another as we follow Him together. His Spirit dwells within us, and as we surrender to that reality, He will flow through us to love others, just like He loves us.

As Partners With God

In addition to living as partners with one another, followers of Jesus have also become partners with God. This partnership is often missed or glossed over in Christian circles because it almost seems too good to be true. Partnering with God in His work, as He sets things right in the world, will become one of the most fulfilling parts of living The 3:30 Life. This sacred partnership bears witness to the Increase of Jesus, because when we get out of the way, God can do what only He could possibly do.

Does God need us to be in partnership with Him? Not at all. As a father myself, I can more clearly understand God's heart when I look at my own children. When I have a project of any size or importance, I don't necessarily need my kids to help me work on it. The truth is that I really enjoy it when they do, and it's even better when they offer to help without my prompting. It's so much more fun to do things together, even though involving them might slow things down for me. But that's okay. I'd rather have the relationship over the speed of the task, any day. When we begin to grasp the reality of a heavenly Father who enjoys accomplishing His plans and purposes together with us, every day becomes an adventure we can't wait to wake up to. Even though we're only bringing "loaves and fish" to the table (Matthew 14:13-21), when those are incorporated into the plans and purposes of God, what happens next will be unpredictable, exhilarating, and mind-blowing. These become milestone moments of immense joy and wonder every single time.

As One

To fully understand the weight of living as partners, we need to push into the threat that's lurking beneath it all. The threat that blurs a clear and beautiful display of Jesus to the world can best be summed up in one word:

Division.

Just before His death, Jesus prayed to His Father, on our behalf. The focus of His prayer was division.

> *"I do not ask for these only, but also for those who will believe*
> *in me through their word, that they may all be one, just as*
> *you, Father, are in me, and I in you, that they also may be in*
> *us, so that the world may believe that you have sent me."*

John 17:20-21

There's so much at stake here. The degree to which we need to be on guard against dividing ourselves in the Body of Christ cannot be overstated. Division among us is evil at its core. If the intention of Jesus is for us to live in unity, then the primary tactic of the enemy is to divide. We see this happening in our families, our churches, our communities, and our nations. If Satan can divide followers of Jesus, causing us to turn against each other, the world will have a harder time believing Jesus was sent from God.

Does being "one" mean that we always agree on everything? Of course not. Living in *unity* does not mean living in *uniformity*. It's not that we won't have strong opinions that result in points of disagreement. It's not that we won't have to work hard at this, or that it will eliminate the need to spend time together allowing our lives to sharpen one another. It simply means that we always place Jesus in the sole place of absolute preeminence, especially above our opinions. He is our common Object of worship, our common Hope of salvation, and our common Giver of grace. If we sense that we're being lured into division, we need to recognize it, confront it, stand firm against it, and overcome it by reminding ourselves of Who gave us our unity in the first place. Paul's words to the church at Ephesus underscore this:

> *"I therefore, a prisoner for the Lord, urge you to walk in a*
> *manner worthy of the calling to which you have been called,*
> *with all humility and gentleness, with patience, bearing with*
> *one another in love, eager to maintain the unity of the Spirit*
> *in the bond of peace. There is one body and one Spirit—just*
> *as you were called to the one hope that belongs to your call—*
> *one Lord, one faith, one baptism, one God and Father of all,*
> *who is over all and through all and in all."*

Ephesians 4:1-6

Conclusion

Back when I was playing, the longest offensive play ever in the history of Stanford football came on a screen pass. I threw the ball behind the line of scrimmage to Glyn Milburn, and after catching it, he ran 92 yards down the field for a touchdown. The pass went as far as most 6-year-olds can throw it. But I did my part, and when I did, it unleashed Glyn to do the very thing he'd been preparing for all year. (And by the way, the other guys on the field did their parts to make that moment possible as well.)

> He is our common Object of worship, our common
> Hope of salvation, and our common Giver of grace.

Often, the things we consider to be insignificant or small end up unlocking the potential for something larger — something we never could have predicted. That's the beauty of living together as partners. It's where God unleashes us and others to live the life He's created us for. When we do so, we discard any individualistic or formulaic mindset, and we embrace something greater. When we refuse to let our disagreements divide us and define us, we begin to experience the beauty of living peacefully and humbly by God's design. At the end of the day, how we live together matters in ways that are larger than we'll ever see, and Paul's words below to the church at Ephesus leave no room for doubt.

"But now in Christ Jesus you who once were far off have been brought near by the blood of Christ. For he himself is our peace, who has made us both one and has broken down in his flesh the dividing wall of hostility by abolishing the law of commandments expressed in ordinances, that he might create in himself one new man in place of the two, so making peace, and might reconcile us both to God in one body through the cross, thereby killing the hostility."

Ephesians 2:13-16

We are partners with each other.

We are partners with God.

We are undivided.

So the world will see and believe.

CHAPTER 15

On Mission

START HERE

SCAN TO WATCH

Living By *DESIGN* Rather Than Default

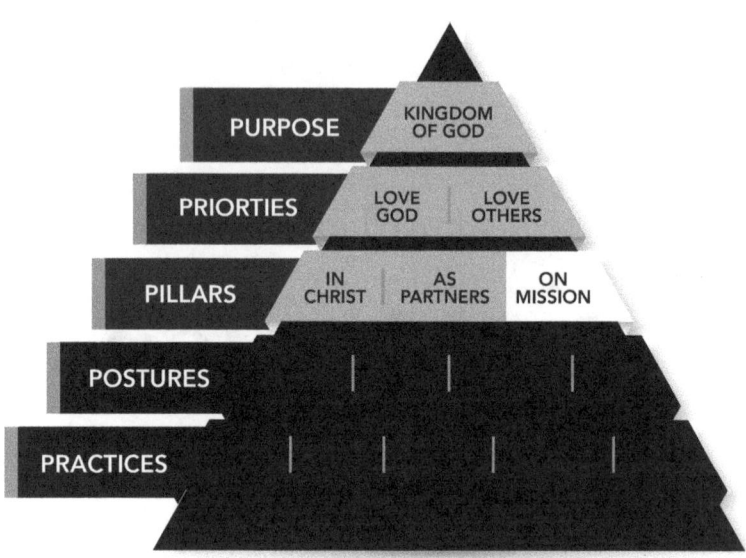

The Three Pillars represent both the realities by which we understand ourselves, and give vocabulary to the bedrock spiritual truths to which we must hold fast. Pillars are the forces that drive us, and the spiritual actualities that inspire us. They support what's theologically true in terms of seeing things with 20/20 vision, and they anchor us firmly into the ground where our feet walk. The third Pillar in The 3:30 Life is the one that identifies our Mission.

We all inherently know what it means to be on a mission. We might say we're on a mission to find the best burger in town or to get in the best shape of our lives. We might be on a team that is resolute in its mission to win the championship. Regardless of what it is, being on mission signifies a deeper level of commitment and determination to succeed in that pursuit.

But what does it mean to be on a mission given to us from God? That's a different question altogether.

What's Our Primary Mission?

To ascertain our primary mission in life, it will be important for us to discover it from the pages of Scripture. It's essential for us to not speculate about this. While it may be tempting for anyone to cherry pick a verse or two from the Bible that aligns with where they already want their mission to take them, we'll need to do better than that. We must adhere to what's true, and we can't get this wrong.

At the end of the Book of Matthew, we encounter some of the final words Jesus spoke to His followers, a talk commonly referred to as "The Great Commission."

> *"And Jesus came and said to them, 'All authority in heaven and on earth has been given to me. Go therefore and make disciples of all nations, baptizing them in the name of the Father and of the Son and of the Holy Spirit, teaching them to observe all that I have commanded you. And behold, I am with you always, to the end of the age.'"*

> Matthew 28:18-20

While volumes have been written about these powerful words, it doesn't take a seminary degree to understand the specifics of the disciples' mission then, and consequently of our mission today. Simply put, we're all to live our lives in such a way that helps the people in our spheres of influence become disciples who also follow in the footsteps of Jesus. How do we do that? We go and live with intentionality wherever we find ourselves, and we endeavor to walk strategically with the people around us until they, too, make their own decision to follow Jesus. We encourage them to be obedient to all that Jesus taught, including a decision to publicly make their faith known to others through the act of baptism. Finally, we must never forget that though there will be times when we feel isolated or insufficient, Jesus is always with us and He has ultimate authority in every situation.

> Simply put, we're all to live our lives in such a way that helps the people in our spheres of influence become disciples who also follow in the footsteps of Jesus.

This is what it looks like to be living a life On Mission, and to live it in close contact with others who bear the image of God. It really is a "co-mission" in partnership with God and others who are *in Christ*. The heart of Jesus was always for people to follow Him, and we are called to simply extend that very same invitation to others as often as we can.

But the story doesn't end there.

At the beginning of the Book of Acts, Luke continues where he left off in his first narrative about Jesus (the Gospel of Luke), and now begins describing what happened as Jesus ascended back into heaven:

> *"But you will receive power when the Holy Spirit has come upon you, and you will be my witnesses in Jerusalem and in all Judea and Samaria, and to the end of the earth.' And when he had said these things, as they were looking on, he was lifted up, and a cloud took him out of their sight."*

Acts 1:8-9

It's the perfect way to describe our primary mission in a nutshell. After Jesus reiterates the promise of His continual presence with His followers (through the work of the Holy Spirit), he tells them that they *will* be witnesses to His life, death, and resurrection. In an age with no internet or cell phones or social media campaigns, Jesus tells His friends that His story will not only be told locally and regionally, but that it will also go to the ends of the earth. Bearing witness to that story must become their lifelong mandate.

> *"And this gospel of the kingdom will be proclaimed*
> *throughout the whole world as a testimony to all nations,*
> *and then the end will come."*

Matthew 24:14

This is the only time Jesus ever declared "and then the end will come." Consider the implications of this. Jesus is declaring that all of human history will reach a critical inflection point when the Gospel is finally declared to the ends of the earth. The narrative of Scripture points toward the glorious Gospel of Jesus going out to all people, in all nations, around the globe. This is the True North of God's mission for every believer, and if we want to be in alignment with the plans and purposes of God's Kingdom, then we can't get distracted from this. For you and me, in the chaos and busyness of our own lives, the words "you will be my witnesses" should leap off the sacred pages of Scripture. Our primary Mission that serves as the third Pillar of The 3:30 Life simply can't be any clearer.

But we all run the risk of getting diverted at times.

Two seasons in the life of King David reveal what happens when we trade a missional life for something lesser. If it could happen to "a man after God's own heart" (1 Samuel 13:14), then I promise — it can happen to any one of us.

A Real-Life Case Study

King David was one of Israel's greatest kings, ultimately included in the lineage of Jesus Himself. We know he defeated Goliath, and we know what that powerful victory did in David's own life and the people as a whole. We know he became king when he was 30 years old and reigned for 40 years. While Scripture tells us that the nation thrived under his leadership, David encountered some major problems in his life as well. Perhaps the most well-known setback was set in motion by one significant domino that fell by David's own choosing.

> *"In the spring of the year, the time when kings go out to*
> *battle, David sent Joab, and his servants with him, and*
> *all Israel. And they ravaged the Ammonites and besieged*
> *Rabbah. But David remained at Jerusalem."*

2 Samuel 11:1

Things are about to completely unravel for the King of Israel. During this season of his life he'll go on to commit adultery, and in an act of power and lust, he'll further his sinful acts by having her husband murdered. David will face massive adversity within his own house and will lose his credibility amongst his royal subjects. He'll remain in denial of his transgressions until God confronts him directly through a prophet. The public will learn of his sin, and the child conceived during his affair will die as an infant.

If you re-read that passage of Scripture, you'll see the conditions were ripe for the temptations and atrocities to take place. A close reading will help us discover what singular event put all other subsequent events into motion: At the time when kings went off to war, David didn't go. Instead, he sent someone else in his place. David lost his mission, and failed to lead like a king should lead. He abandoned the work God had given him to complete, and opted instead for personal safety and the fulfillment of his selfish desires. David traded He for Me. It's not difficult to identify the underlying themes of comfort, accomplishment, ambition, security, prosperity, and competing worldviews as they bubble to the surface of this story.

While we may not make the exact same mistakes David made, we're certainly never exempt from the temptation of trading our primary Mission for something lesser. For some of us it may be time to pivot from a lifestyle that chases after temporal pursuits, which leaves us endlessly yearning for more and more and more. Please keep in mind God is always redeeming and restoring that which is lost. He did exactly that with David. Was it Plan A? Probably not. But despite all David had done, there was an eventual rekindling of the relationship he once had with God, and that he once had with Israel.

I hope you're hearing this loud and clear: It's never too late to start or restart living On Mission, no matter what your life has looked like in the past. There's a reason the windshield is far bigger than the rearview mirror, and that's because what's in front of us is far more significant than what's behind. So if you're inspired to live a life on God's Mission, then what comes next can't be overemphasized.

EXPERT WITNESS OR EYEWITNESS?

What does it mean for us to live On Mission — to be a witness to the life of Jesus, and to live our days following in His footsteps? There was a season in my life when I desperately desired to be Christ's witness to the world around me, yet I was also wrestling with the realization that I couldn't always answer everyone's many questions about Jesus. Or the authority of Scripture. Or the Trinity. Or a host of other things about Christianity. At times, I think we all have felt that way.

> There's a reason the windshield is far bigger than the rearview mirror, and that's because what's in front of us is far more significant than what's behind.

A mentor of mine helped me in this journey by showing me a distinction that set me free. He pointed out that, in a court of law, there are *expert witnesses*, and there are *eyewitnesses*. I had spent way too long thinking that I needed to become an expert witness about all things Jesus before I started telling others about His life-transforming power. But my mentor said, "Steve, keep growing and keep following Jesus. Don't wait until you have all the answers. You are an eyewitness to the saving grace of Christ in your life, and you can share that now, even though you're not an expert witness."

When he said that, I was set free and also inspired to adopt a new posture of willingness. I realized the perspective of someone who's walking with Jesus (and going where He leads) is the absolute willingness to bear witness to the story of Jesus, His life, and saving grace. Our witness to others begins with a retelling of our Great Exchange story (as discussed and defined in Chapter 4), and must include some portion of that moment when we went from death to life, as best as we can recall it. We're talking about the time you made a resolute decision to follow Jesus — to say, "No matter where everyone else is going, I'm following Him." We tell our story because it's our eyewitness account of what's happened as a result of our encounter with Christ.

In John 9, Jesus heals a blind man, and it's a story you'll want to read in its entirety. After Jesus heals him, people take notice of the changes in this man's life and he immediately faces a series of questions from his neighbors, others who knew him previously as a blind beggar, and ultimately the religious leaders. Even his parents were brought in to help understand what had happened and to clarify that he was, indeed, a person who had been blind from birth. The intensity of the scene grows as the religious leaders try to pressure the man into becoming an expert witness. They want him to not only confirm that his eyesight has been restored, but also to explain things about Jesus that he is not yet qualified to do. "Tell the truth about this," they demanded. A complete reading of the story in John 9 actually feels like a courtroom. In the end, the healed man's pithy yet powerful response stopped his accusers dead in their tracks, and still echoes today for *all* who have become eyewitnesses to the mighty acts of God: "One thing I do know, that though I was blind, now I see" (John 9:25).

The story of the blind man should inspire us. What if that story became a starting point for us to navigate the details of bearing witness to our Jesus story? Does every conversation we have with others need to begin with, "I need to share my faith with you right now"? Absolutely not. But there needs to be an awareness that the most important story we'll ever tell people is about Jesus — about what He's accomplished on our behalf, how that's given us abundant life now, as well as eternal life forever. Do we need to have every answer to every spiritual question?

Not at all. I can't tell you how many times I've responded with, "That's a great question. I'll need to get back to you on that one. There are people who are more knowledgeable than me who already know the answer." In those discussions, I'm an *eyewitness* who recognizes my limited abilities to be an *expert witness*. And in those moments — especially in those moments — I'm grateful to know there are expert witnesses who can provide me with understanding and answers to ultimately circle back with those who were asking.

At the end of the day, we need to be relatable and loving people who care about the well-being of those around us. When we live with the Two Priorities of loving God and loving others, it's easy to see that bearing witness to the Jesus story will always involve both our words and our actions. The totality of our lives should speak volumes through the way we live, and through the testimony of Jesus in the words we speak. We should act and speak in a compelling and winsome manner, to the point that the people around us will ask us about the hope they see in us (1 Peter 3:15). Our lives should provoke questions from those who are on the receiving end of the grace we display ... and also from those who are watching it all from a distance.

When we choose to enter the world where it's hurting the most, we're confronted by our own limitations, and we're forced to depend on a provision that goes far beyond our own abilities. Hurting people are looking for help and listening more than ever before. If we will intentionally engage with others in this way, we'll be representing His Kingdom wherever He's sovereignly placed us, and we'll be responding to Christ's mandate to love others holistically within our spheres of influence. With the following words from the Book of John as our guide we allow compassion, rather than condemnation, to motivate us: "For God did not send his Son into the world to condemn the world, but in order that the world might be saved through him" (John 3:17).

The story of Jesus is not only the best story to tell, it's also the most compelling story people will ever hear. And make no mistake — it's the life we're invited to live, and to share.

CONCLUSION

The Three Pillars that support the best lives we can possibly live are:

Pillar #1: In Christ.

Pillar #2: As Partners.

Pillar #3: On Mission.

In Christ, our identities are secure, and our being precedes our doing. As Partners, we accomplish abundantly more for God's Kingdom as we serve together. As we live On Mission, the story of Jesus is told through our lives, in both word and deed.

The life of God will be discovered in these three Pillars, and will always provide us with everything we need to support our 3:30 Life.

This is a life that happens when we live by design, rather than default.

CHAPTER 16

Postures

START HERE

SCAN TO WATCH

Living By *DESIGN* Rather Than Default

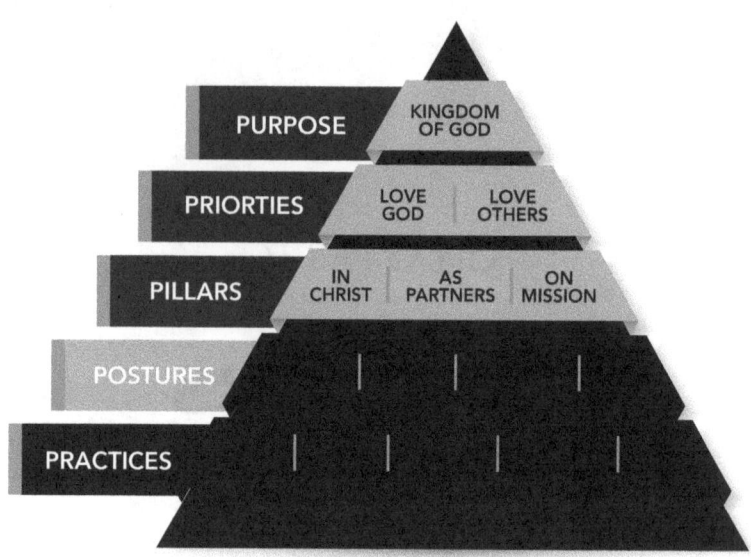

My past experience as a professional quarterback now allows me the privilege of spending time with younger quarterbacks, coaching and teaching them the things I've learned over the years. When I train a young QB, it's far more than simply playing catch, or taking them through a predictable series of drills. Instead, as I begin my evaluation, I start by assessing their readiness, taking into account their current level of development and skill. As I do so, my assessment ultimately boils down to four key data points. It's these four things that will maximize their potential, and increase the likelihood of eventually completing passes in real game situations when it matters most. And when I see these four indicators, I know they're ready.

First, I'm looking at their *foot position*, making sure their back foot is loaded properly and they're driving maximum force into the ground. Second, I'm looking at their *hip position*, because that's where any true throwing motion starts. Third, I'm looking at the *ball position*, making sure it's not too far forward or backward, too high or too low. And finally, I'm looking at their *eye position*, ensuring they are both looking up as well as downfield. All four of these postures will ultimately result in a quarterback being prepared and ready.

Why are they so important? Because when quarterbacks get into a game situation, the speed and the intensity encountered on the field will demand that their instincts take over. This reality is only compounded when you add in the schemes and tactics of the defense. As a result, in game situations quarterbacks can't be thinking about whether they're ready or not. They just need to play.

What's true in football can, again, provide a helpful metaphor for all of us living The 3:30 Life. A life of design and intention requires us to be actively in the moments of our lives, not passively waiting in the stands or on the sidelines. We're in the game of life, and the reality of this game is that the speed and intensity we experience don't allow us to predict what will happen next. We must be both proactive in our approach, as well as ready to react effectively when unexpected elements unfold. Similar to the football metaphor, this is only compounded and confused by the attacks the enemy will send our way. The defense on the field is taking the same proactive and intentional approach in their opposition to our efforts. Concisely stated, if we're not prepared and ready, our full potential won't be unleashed, and our ability to complete our assignments will be minimized.

Postures are ultimately an indicator of preparation and readiness.

> A life of design and intention requires us to be actively in the moments of our lives, not passively waiting in the stands or on the sidelines.

THE FOUR POSTURES

There are many postures that position us for a life of following Jesus — for a life of preparedness and unlocked potential — but I've narrowed them down to four. In the same way I look at the four postures mentioned previously for any young QB, there are also postures I look for in myself (or in another person) as evidence of a readiness to live The 3:30 Life. Even though we'll spend the next four chapters leaning into each Posture with care and intention, identifying them here will galvanize our journey as we move from Me to He.

The orientation of the first two Postures refers to the relationship between *God* and *ourselves*:

Posture #1: Surrender

Posture #2: Worship

The orientation of the last two postures refers to the relationship between *ourselves* and *others*:

Posture #3: Community

Posture #4: Service

By definition, all four are Decrease postures, meaning the more we humble ourselves in them the better. They require us to move away from Me, and reorient ourselves toward He, and toward others. The more consistent and more stable we become in these four areas, the more likely we are to experience the Increase of Christ in our pursuit of The 3:30 Life.

However, before we move on, it's important to frame the conversation about Postures accurately. Postures are something we *work toward*, but that doesn't mean we ever *completely arrive at them*. They're the picture of the ideal state for Christ followers to fully unlock our potential, and they're dynamic journeys rather than static destinations. Postures should encourage us rather than discourage us, motivate us rather than frustrate us. I'd never want any reader to come away from these chapters with the impression that I've mastered the Four Postures, but rather to understand that I'm simply on the journey with you. The critical distinction here is that postures are still a description of our being, rather than a prescription for our doing.

MOTIVATED FOR READINESS

Maintaining a picture of the Four Postures in our minds will continually motivate us and focus us in what we choose to do during the minutes and hours of our lives. Preparing for any significant endeavor requires hard work. Athletes who train alone in the dark every morning know this all too well. Most athletes strategically place pictures or posters in their surroundings of those they hope to emulate as they pursue their craft. Those pictures inform how they get ready through practice and hard work when no one is looking, and those same pictures serve as affirmation along the journey when they see more and more similarities between themselves and the images they have chosen to fixate on.

The same is true for those who are following Jesus and who desire to experience His Increase more and more in their daily lives. There must be some greater truth that pulls us into the motivation we need to live The 3:30 Life. There must be "pictures" we hope to emulate that will increasingly unlock our potential to live the life God intended when He made us. Postures are those pictures.

I believe there are two primary truths that will motivate us to do the intentional and disciplined work of preparing ourselves for a life of Christ's Increase.

First, we're motivated as we live by design. The inspiration to be game-ready happens when we live by design, not by default. As we've discussed already, we're a unique workmanship that God has created (Ephesians 2:10), and have all been given a unique race to run by the Author Himself (Hebrews 12:1). So if God has created us with the handiwork of a master craftsman, and if He's given us a race to run that's equally one-of-a-kind, then why wouldn't we want to spend time preparing for everything that might make us ready to travel our specific journey ahead?

Secondly, we're motivated as we focus on the finish line. We've all heard the phrase, "Begin with the end in mind." In pursuit of The 3:30 Life, we might adjust it to say, "Live with the end in mind." As discussed in Psalm 90, Moses reminds us that our days are finite and brief. Scripture is clear that we will spend far more time in heaven beyond our days on earth, and the quality of that experience will be influenced by what we do while we are here. There will be an evaluation moment for each of us when life is over (Romans 14:10; 1 Corinthians 5:9) or when Jesus returns for those still living (Revelation 22:12). Staying focused on what will impact our eternity will motivate us to live in alignment with God's Kingdom purpose during our days.

SUSTAINED FOR THE JOURNEY

While it's vital that we adopt the proper motivations for living The 3:30 Life, there's a challenging question that presents itself as a part of this larger conversation. Anyone can *begin* the journey with Jesus, but how can we continue and *complete* it? The Apostle Paul addresses the same question in his letter to the Colossian believers:

"Therefore, as you received Christ Jesus the Lord, so walk in him, rooted and built up in him and established in the faith, just as you were taught, abounding in thanksgiving."

Colossians 2:6-7

> They'll position us toward a life of He, and away from the absurdity of a life of Me.

How can we be sustained for this journey? It's easy for any of us to adopt an event-based approach to our faith, where we learn to depend solely on the next external inputs to carry us through the day-in and day-out realities of life. While events are significant and can inspire us, they are limited in their capacity to help us follow through on our good intentions. Paul reminds us that we are to "walk in him, rooted and built up in him and established in the faith." Once again, the source that sustains us is Him. It's internal rather than external, and it's found in our daily walk with Jesus far more than in the weekly, monthly, or yearly events we attend. If what is most needed is a sustainable approach to The Following, then I can say this with absolute certainty...

The ongoing cultivation of these four Postures will become what enables you to sustain the life that God has created you for.

Postures are the bridge between our "moments of inspiration" and the "established life of faith" required for us to see victory in the real world.

CONCLUSION

We're on the ground now. We're in the game. Postures are, by nature, designed to get us ready for our daily lives, and they take us beyond our good intentions. After you're finished reading this, you'll walk out the door, or head to your home office, or jump into your role as mom or dad, and you won't have any way of knowing what's about to happen next. The pace and the intensity of life will hit us, and if we're not prepared, we'll get swept away.

Isn't it time to live deeply in the moments of your life without getting swept away?

Postures will prepare us for that. They'll position us toward a life of He, and away from the absurdity of a life of Me. And as we cultivate them, we'll position ourselves to experience the Increase moments that only God can create, lived with the humility and dependence that pleases Him most.

This is the life you were created for.

CHAPTER 17

Surrender

START HERE

SCAN TO WATCH

Living By *DESIGN* Rather Than Default

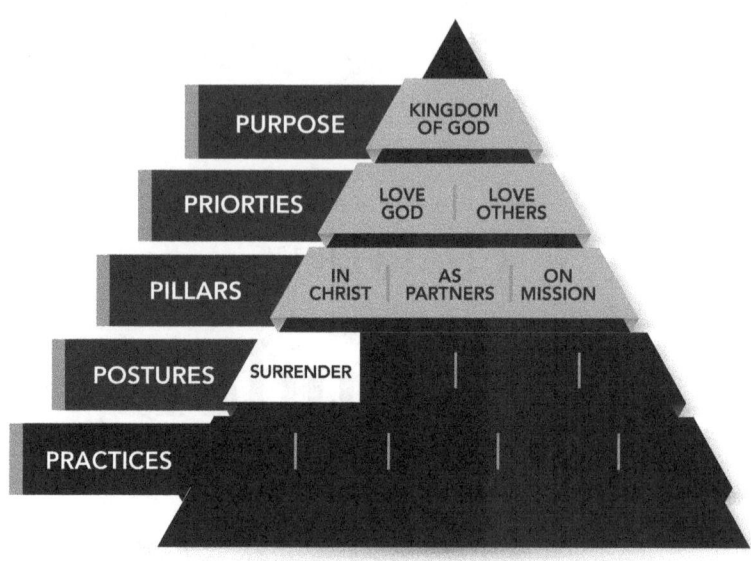

As we continue the process of learning how to live The 3:30 Life, we're discovering that there are certain Postures to embrace. The ongoing cultivation of these Postures enables us to live the abundant Life that God has created us for. Postures ready us for the complexities and challenges of life, and give us the potential to experience the Increase of Jesus during those special moments when we get out of the way, and He shows up.

The first Posture is Surrender.

Webster defines surrender as "yielding to the power, control, or possession of another upon compulsion or demand." Throughout history, a common symbol of surrender has been waving a white flag. The color white indicated that a person had voluntarily removed himself from the act of fighting — that no more blood would be spilled. Soldiers would literally open their hands as they watched their swords or guns fall to the ground, and then wave a white flag in surrender.

For anyone who has authentically decided to follow Jesus, these stories and metaphors should make sense. With open hands, we're raising a white flag of surrender to God, not just once, but daily. In these moments, we're making a choice to release the power we think we have — not to an enemy who fights *against* us, but instead to a sovereign God who fights *for* us. It's easy to see why Christians have adopted the word "surrender," and have made it a part of our everyday language.

> It's an intentional letting go of any claim we've staked over our lives, and a willingness to become fully available to God.

Sometimes, surrendering is easier said than done. If we're honest with ourselves, we can sometimes resist raising the white flag, because posturing ourselves toward surrender makes us feel weak. Or conquered. Or out of control. And who wants to feel that?

In reality, raising any white flag of surrender is diametrically opposed to what most of us have been taught our entire lives. From day one, we've been encouraged to become the best version of ourselves, and the culture around us celebrates anything we do that helps us develop into *that* person. We're affirmed when we muscle our way through the difficult events of our lives, so we learn habits of conquering and achieving through our own efforts. We then tell the stories of our victories, even when they're vaguely concealed in our statements of false humility. By default we assume a posture that stakes a claim over our own lives, and the cultural currents all around us only reinforce the pull-ourselves-up-by-our-bootstraps approach to life. In the end, living in a default-reality that mirrors almost everyone else around us allows us the perception of being in control over our actions, our beliefs, our decisions and our accomplishments.

It's a vicious cycle and it's not the life we are designed to live. The great news is God not only saves us from what we will do by default, He invites us into the very life He intends.

Release - The Heartbeat of Surrender

Set the book down, make a fist as tight as you can, then slowly release your grip. That's what surrender feels like. It's experienced in our release of those things we're holding onto tightly. It's something we need to do multiple times every day, to the point that it becomes innate. Real surrender is the opposite of grasping and hoarding. It's an intentional letting go of any claim we've staked over our lives, and a willingness to become fully available to God.

"Or do you not know that your body is a temple of the
Holy Spirit within you, whom you have from God?
You are not your own, for you were bought with a price.
So glorify God in your body."

1 Corinthians 6:19-20

Our lives have been bought back by God. We're not our own; we now belong to Him. While that new reality ultimately frees us, surrendering to it will require times when we must choose where our trust resides.

No one knew this better than Abraham.

ABRAHAM - A PORTRAIT OF SURRENDER

Even though Abraham would become the "Father of Nations," he was also a dad. In Genesis 22, God invites Abraham into a surrender story that would continue to be told for every generation to come.

"After these things God tested Abraham and said to him, 'Abraham!' And he said, 'Here I am.'

"He said, 'Take your son, your only son Isaac, whom you love, and go to the land of Moriah, and offer him there as a burnt offering on one of the mountains of which I shall tell you.'"

Genesis 22:1-2

While it's natural for us to ask, "What kind of a God does this?" the writer of Genesis doesn't answer that question. Rather, as the story continues, he answers the real question we should all be asking: "What kind of a person says 'yes' to this?"

The answer?

A person who's fully surrendered.

If you were to name the top five heroes of the faith in Scripture, Abraham's name would most certainly be there. Every New Testament writer who wrote about Jesus understood the role Abraham played, but it's possible for us to set him on a pedestal — one that's not merited, given his humanity. Even though Abraham represented the family through which the Messiah would come, he was still just a person nonetheless. Like John the Baptist years later, Abraham isn't a bronze statue to behold, but a man who had so much confidence in God that he was compelled to trust Him with complete open-handedness.

Surrender was already Abraham's posture long before he traveled the road to Moriah.

You probably know the rest of the story. Abraham and his son arrived at the place God had made known to them. Abraham built the altar, bound his son Isaac, and laid him on top of it. At the apex of the story, we read:

> *"Then Abraham reached out his hand and took the knife*
> *to slaughter his son. But the angel of the Lord called to him*
> *from heaven and said, 'Abraham, Abraham!'*

> *"And he said, 'Here I am.'*

> *"He said, 'Do not lay your hand on the boy or do anything to*
> *him, for now I know that you fear God, seeing you have not*
> *withheld your son, your only son, from me.'"*

Genesis 22:10-12

The story continues and the tension is resolved when a substitute ram is provided as a sacrifice in place of Abraham's only son. This is clearly a foreshadowing of Jesus who, as God's only Son, becomes "the Lamb ... who takes away the sin of the world" (John 1:29).

Hundreds of years later, looking back on this monumental event in Abraham's life, the writer of Hebrews gives us a glimpse into what Abraham thought would happen.

"He considered that God was able even to raise him
from the dead..."

Hebrews 11:19

That's how surrendered to God Abraham was. Even if the unthinkable had happened to his son Isaac, Abraham had already conceived of a way for God to rescue the situation.

A Posture of Surrender invites us all to lean into the faith that Abraham displayed. Our vantage point at the beginning of any surrender moment will never allow us to see the fullness of His desired outcome. In those moments, a simple "yes" is all that's required.

ALLEGIANCE - THE FRUIT OF SURRENDER

If you've been in church or around many Christians, you'll hear these verses quoted regularly:

"And whoever does not take his cross and follow me is not
worthy of me. Whoever finds his life will lose it, and whoever
loses his life for my sake will find it."

Matthew 10:38-39

The Posture of Surrender is truly at the heart of the life that Jesus invites us into. There's a strong correlation between The Following and the cross. When Jesus said the words "take up their cross," anyone within earshot would have known exactly what He was saying. This wasn't a metaphor for His listeners, but a brutal reality they'd witnessed in the lives of people who'd dared to challenge Rome. Often the people who were subject to taking up their cross, at least in the time of Jesus, were people who were a threat to Roman rule, because their allegiance was to a leader other than Caesar.

So when Jesus chose those words, His hearers would have been faced with one life-altering question: Where is my allegiance?

There is only one appropriate answer: A Christ follower's allegiance will always be only to God.

That's a Posture of Surrender.

JESUS - THE OBJECT OF SURRENDER

The Posture of Surrender and the Object of our surrender go hand in hand. When Jesus declares the words above about following Him, He's not speaking as a verbally aggressive general in the armed services. He's not speaking as an angry dad in a toxic household, nor is He speaking as an all-powerful authoritarian leader. Even though His words are difficult to hear, Jesus always remains full of grace and truth as He speaks (John 1:11). He's been given to the world by a good and loving Father on a rescue mission to chase us down, and to invite us to come home. We must remember this, or risk obsessing over a set of rules rather than embracing a relationship with God Himself and discovering the fullness of life as He has designed it.

While we should always view God with a healthy reverence, our Posture of Surrender is predicated on His goodness and faithfulness. The general, the angry dad, and the authoritarian leader all *require* the allegiance of the people around them, but surrender to those leaders is based on the fear of what might happen if they don't. God doesn't relate to us that way. When we open our clenched hands and release everything to Him, then we'll discover Him to be good and kind, full of purpose and redemption. In doing so, we place ourselves in a posture that's primed to experience all that "God has prepared for those who love him" (1 Corinthians 2:9).

Is it Time to Quit?

I'm making the claim that true surrender to God will run antithetical to everything we've been taught. Our culture tells us to never quit, and to never surrender. It's an underlying theme found in the books we read, and often in the sermons we hear. So many good people have been seduced by the illusion of their own control. But if a Posture of Surrender feels like quitting to you, then maybe it's time to just quit. While our instincts will be to try to work even harder by our own strength, I encourage you to rest in the God who is truly in control of your life. Maybe waving a white flag is the thing your heart has been crying out for all along, but wasn't apparent until now. Maybe it's the perfect time to release the past you can't let go of, the present you're trying to push through, or the future you're trying to create. What if the surrendered posture of Jesus becomes yours too?

"Nevertheless, not my will, but yours, be done."

Luke 22:42

> Maybe it's the perfect time to release the past you can't let go of, the present you're trying to push through, or the future you're trying to create.

CONCLUSION

I know how difficult this can be. If you're like me, you can't help but feel the tension that a Posture of Surrender requires of us. In one direction, we're being pulled toward the extravagant and compelling love of God. In the other direction, we're having to let go of ownership over our own lives. The following verses illuminate this tension:

"See what kind of love the Father has given to us, that we should be called children of God; and so we are."

1 John 3:1

"You are not your own, for you were bought with a price."

1 Corinthians 6:19-20

I invite you to sit in that tension before you move on to the next thing that's pulling at you. Be courageous as you do so. Take as long as you need, close your eyes, and simply repeat these words:

"God, You have lavished me with Your love. I am not my own. I belong to You"

...and again...

"God, You have lavished me with Your love. I am not my own. I belong to You"

...and a third time, slowly, and thoughtfully...

"God, You have lavished me with Your love. I am not my own. I belong to You"

For the healthy and the sick, the rich and the poor, the powerful and the powerless, it's these words that best express an open-handed release, and a waving of the white flag. In all the seasons of our lives, we simply do our very best, then leave the results in His hands. When our hearts are thirsty to experience the presence and the pleasure of God, we approach our lives with a wide-eyed expectation that God will make Himself known to us.

So open your hands today. And then again tomorrow. And then again the next day. You won't believe the ways you'll see the Kingdom of God from this front row seat.

CHAPTER 18

Worship

START HERE

SCAN TO WATCH

Living By *DESIGN* Rather Than Default

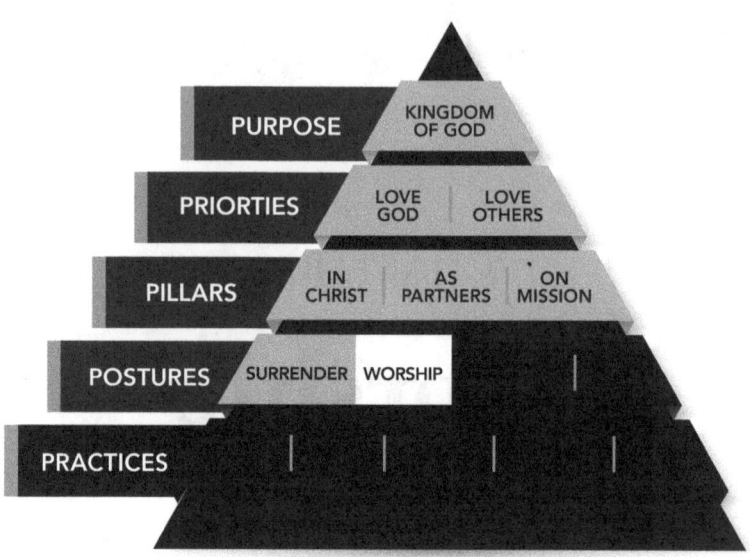

Every Posture we're exploring is a posture of decrease. They all represent an intentional orientation of self that pushes away from Me, and awakens us more fully to a life of He. They equip us to experience the very essence of The 3:30 Life, and like a player on the field who's maximizing their readiness for the game, the Postures position us to be intuitively prepared for anything in our day-to-day lives that comes our way. These truths apply to all four Postures, but are perhaps brought to life most fully when we experience the Posture of Worship.

First Things First

We were made to worship, and we're really quite good at it. That's because it's natural for us to continually ascribe worth to someone or something. We don't really need to try because it's almost automatic ... intuitive even. If we're honest with ourselves, we've been doing this all our lives, whether we call it worship or not.

While we are all made to worship, we are also made NOT to be worshiped.

All throughout the Scriptures, the writers intentionally craft their words so their hearers know Who is worthy of worship, and who is not. They believe that worship is more than something we do, and that it actually extends into a Posture we take. One of the most appropriate starting points for any discussion about worship is found at the very beginning of the Ten Commandments.

"And God spoke all these words, saying, 'I am the Lord your God, who brought you out of the land of Egypt, out of the house of slavery. You shall have no other gods before me.'"

Exodus 20:1-3

While there will be nine more commandments, and even more after that, there's a reason the first commandment spoken by God has everything to do with the Object of our worship. It's because the One who created us knows how strongly our hearts are pulled toward worshiping, and how our lives are saturated with gods all around us who lure us in. In His infinite wisdom, God beats us to the punch.

"You shall have no other gods before me."

These days, we don't tend to think about worship in connection with gods or idols. If we're committed to placing first things first, then we need to talk about gods, and as we have this discussion, you'll notice that it's intentionally written with a lowercase "g."

The most obvious gods that creep into our lives come from the outside. We create gods out of our favorite athletes and celebrities. We look to our political leaders as messiah figures who will save the day, or fall into the trap of idolizing our country of origin. The gods of money and fortune might be found at the top of our lists, while the perceived status of our resumes and titles can also be given more weight than they ought.

> However, our tendency is to take these gifts, and turn them into something more than they can carry, and ascribe more worth to them than they can fulfill.

There are also gods that live on the inside, and can be a little less obvious. Our desires can lead us to create idols out of our spouses and our children. Our health can easily become something we worship, and achievement can easily turn into another god. We might gravitate toward the allure of sex, the acquisition of knowledge, or the power we think we have to influence the world around us.

The interesting thing about these gods is that many of them can be very good things. Reread the list of everything mentioned above, and you'll see that they, in their best form, can all be gifts from God. However, our tendency is to take these gifts, and turn them into something more than they can carry, and ascribe more worth to them than they can fulfill. If we don't recognize these as gifts by design, then they will, by default, become idols.

Why is God so intentional and absolute about making this commandment the first thing out of His mouth? For starters, God is adamant that He will not share His glory with another. It's hard to miss the roar of His voice when He says...

"I am the Lord; that is my name;
my glory I give to no other,
nor my praise to carved idols."

Isaiah 42:8

And for many of you, that's all you need to hear.

In reading this passage, we're also compelled to abandon our idols because it's clearly God's way of protecting us. Idol worship is heavy, and it always disappoints. When we continually default to the worship of our idols, and when we pursue people and systems who will make idols out of us, that worship will always lead to our own demise. If we discover our value based on the amount of followers we have, then we're only putting Me back onto the seat of worship. We're sucked into something for which we're not made, and the weight of it all will absolutely crush us. No one is made for that, and the amount of people who have been crushed under the weight of their own adoration and praise serves as a sobering reminder of how dangerous worshiping oneself can be.

So how do we position our lives to put first things first, and to worship the only One who is of highest magnitude? If we already know the character of God disallows all other gods, and if we know He's protecting us from our own demise at the same time, then how do we reorient the Posture of our lives around His supremacy and His care?

"But seek first the kingdom of God and his righteousness, and all these things
will be added to you."

Matthew 6:33

As we saw in Chapter 7, this verse reminds us that pursuing our singular purpose is always the answer. It's one thing to memorize these words of Jesus, but it's another thing to spend a lifetime intentionally unpacking how they apply to every aspect of our lives. If The 3:30 Life is inviting us into anything, it's inviting us into a life with our eyes wide open.

It's inviting us to see.

LEARNING TO SEE

We worship our idols because we can see them. They're in our social feeds, on our streaming devices, and all around us each day. God understands this about us, and knows full well that making Him our sole Object of worship requires faith in Someone unseen.

The Gospel writer John — the very same disciple who may have been Jesus' closest friend — was exiled by Rome to an island called Patmos. As he grew older and wiser, he had a vision, and his words are recorded in what is now known as the Book of Revelation. In the powerful vision God gave to John, he describes the scene of heaven. Without getting caught up in the identities of those involved, I believe we've been given a passage of Scripture to help us see the God who's at the center of everything:

> *"After this I looked, and behold, a door standing open in*
> *heaven! And the first voice, which I had heard speaking to*
> *me like a trumpet, said, 'Come up here, and I will show you*
> *what must take place after this.' At once I was in the Spirit,*
> *and behold, a throne stood in heaven, with one seated on the*
> *throne. And he who sat there had the appearance of jasper and*
> *carnelian, and around the throne was a rainbow that had the*

appearance of an emerald. Around the throne were twenty-four thrones, and seated on the thrones were twenty-four elders, clothed in white garments, with golden crowns on their heads. From the throne came flashes of lightning, and rumblings and peals of thunder, and before the throne were burning seven torches of fire, which are the seven spirits of God, and before the throne there was as it were a sea of glass, like crystal.

"And around the throne, on each side of the throne, are four living creatures, full of eyes in front and behind: the first living creature like a lion, the second living creature like an ox, the third living creature with the face of a man, and the fourth living creature like an eagle in flight. And the four living creatures, each of them with six wings, are full of eyes all around and within, and day and night they never cease to say,

"'Holy, holy, holy, is the Lord God Almighty, who was and is and is to come!'

"And whenever the living creatures give glory and honor and thanks to him who is seated on the throne, who lives forever and ever, the twenty-four elders fall down before him who is seated on the throne and worship him who lives forever and ever. They cast their crowns before the throne, saying,

"'Worthy are you, our Lord and God, to receive glory and honor and power, for you created all things, and by your will they existed and were created.'"

Revelation 4:1-11

That's the God we worship. *That's* the God whose beauty and wonder compels us to lay down any crowns of our own making, or any idols of our own choosing. *That's* the God who we fall on our faces before, filled with more awe and gratitude than human languages can convey.

John's vision takes us beyond what our minds can grasp on their own. Faith is required, and faith allows us to see God as we position ourselves toward Him as our only Object of worship. As our lives bend toward the throne of God as described in Revelation, the only appropriate response becomes something that bursts forth from our hearts as an exhale of praise.

THE EXHALE OF PRAISE

If a Posture of Surrender is best seen as an opening of our clenched fists, then a Posture of Worship raises those same opened hands, and exhales praise to Him. While surrender involves forfeiting our claim to everything, worship involves bringing everything to Him. These are the moments when all the things burdening us fade into the background. The worries of this life — those thorns and thistles that have taken root — are now in the back seat, and God Himself gets elevated to every high place. We experience gratitude and thanksgiving for all that He is, and for everything He's done. We know we're in a Posture of Worship when gratitude for every good gift is continually experienced as we ascribe ultimate worth back to God. These verses from Psalm 96 illustrate what that means:

> *"Ascribe to the Lord, O families of the peoples, ascribe to the*
> *Lord glory and strength!*
> *Ascribe to the Lord the glory due his name; bring an*
> *offering, and come into his courts!*
> *Worship the Lord in the splendor of holiness;*

tremble before him, all the earth!
Say among the nations, 'The Lord reigns!'"

Psalm 96:7-10

CONCLUSION

So let's make this personal. If we're caught up in the spin cycle of worshiping idols, then here's a simple question to ask yourself that will take you out of the spin, and into something that's intensely relevant:

What's the allure behind the worship you give to your idols?

Is it because you're *inspired* by them? What if instead, you became inspired only by GOD?

Is it because you're *enamored* by them? What would it take for you to immerse yourself in the Scriptures with the goal of allowing the love of GOD to overwhelm you?

Is it because you want to *mimic* your object of worship, or to become like it? What if you allow the life of JESUS to live through you, so that you become more like Him each day?

Is it because you enjoy the *accolades* that come your way? What would it take for you to grab every accolade and exhale it with gratitude toward GOD, giving that worth back to Him?

The best place to start is always with Jesus, and there may be no greater passage of Scripture that gets us into a Posture of Worship than in Paul's letter to the Colossian church. As you read these words, allow them to become your exhale. Be unedited and unashamed. Be declarative and bold. And more than anything...

Be grateful.

> *"He is the image of the invisible God, the firstborn of all creation. For by him all things were created, in heaven and on earth, visible and invisible, whether thrones or dominions or rulers or authorities—all things were created through him and for him. And he is before all things, and in him all things hold together. And he is the head of the body, the church. He is the beginning, the firstborn from the dead, that in everything he might be preeminent. For in him all the fullness of God was pleased to dwell, and through him to reconcile to himself all things, whether on earth or in heaven, making peace by the blood of his cross."*

Colossians 1:15-20

May you remain with these words, and may these words remain with you. May the Posture of Worship toward the ONE TRUE GOD become the greatest pursuit of your life. May you learn to see God as He truly is, and may you ascribe worth back to Him as your exhale of praise. May you discover the fruit of gratitude, and the fullest possible joy in His presence.

And by the grace of God, may you experience the awe and wonder of every new day, of every good gift, and of every redeemed moment spent with the God who chased you down, and brought you home.

CHAPTER 19

Community

START HERE

SCAN TO WATCH

Living By *DESIGN* Rather Than Default

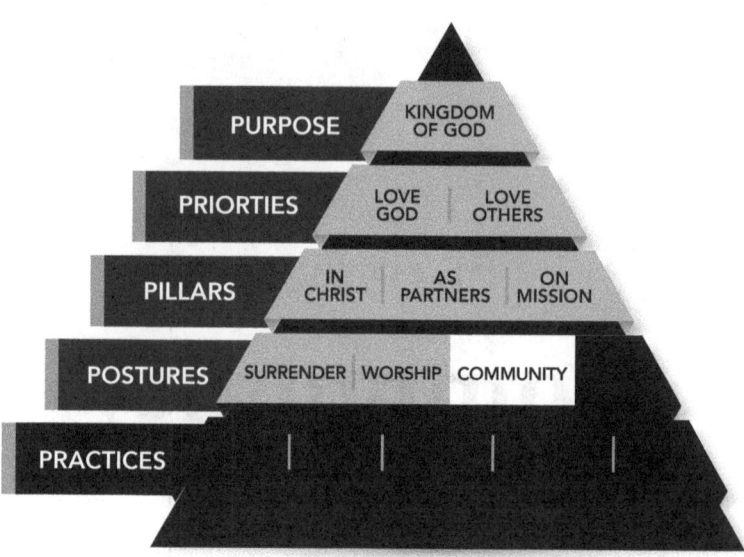

People often ask me what it was like to be inside an actual NFL huddle. My answer is always the same: "There's nothing quite like it." There are moments of congratulations and high-fives, but also times of frustration and confusion because the schemes of the defense are working against us. The huddle pulls us back together, allows us to take inventory, and then helps us map out the best next course of action.

Who doesn't want their own version of that? We all want those moments of high-fives and celebration, no matter how big or how small. Everyone desires a safe place to express their frustration or confusion, and then to lean on others for help. Additionally, we all would benefit from having a space to receive the encouragement that allows us to persevere when facing strong opposition.

Everyone wants that.

But it's not that easy, is it? The systems that are now firmly embedded in our culture stand in direct opposition to our innate need for community. With one click of a button, we can get everything we think we "need" from other people, yet without any actual face-to-face contact, and without ever even venturing outside our home. A lifestyle like this can, over time, create a belief system where the value of others becomes primarily transactional, concerned only with what we can get *from* them. It's objective, quantifiable, and requires no real relationship. We are connected *to* each other in a myriad of ways, but we are not connected *with* each other in the most important ways.

> What we need most is the huddle, but we settle for the internet. Thank God the writers of Scripture paint a much different picture!

And that's only what we see on the surface. What's happening beneath the surface, I believe, is our own growing acceptance of a posture of individualism. It's alluring for most people to be recognized as "independent." We don't *really* believe we need others, and a life of independence is the fruit of that belief. The entrepreneurial spirit can be beautiful and powerful because it allows people to chase their dreams and passions, but when it crosses a line into a declaration of not needing others, then our souls will never be truly satisfied. Far too many of us find ourselves isolated in crowds, when what we need is connection in community.

In addition, we keep bumping into the reality of an enemy — an adversary who wants to take us out. He schemes to lure us into isolation, and like a fish that believes the bait is real, we readily accept individualism as something good and virtuous. Our enemy repeatedly whispers these lies to us, and if we're not posturing ourselves toward real community, then a snowball effect ensues, leaving us on a wide road that culminates in hopelessness and defeat. Solomon recognized this when he said, "And though a man might prevail against one who is alone, two will withstand him—a threefold cord is not quickly broken" (Ecclesiastes 4:12).

The reality is tragic: We're drifting, and we have been for some time. We're slowly and incrementally moving away from a Posture of Community, and choosing instead to posture ourselves toward individualism and isolation.

What we need most is the huddle, but we settle for the internet. Thank God the writers of Scripture paint a much different picture!

> Far too many of us find ourselves isolated in crowds,
> when what we need is connection in community.

THE MODEL OF COMMUNITY

The life of Jesus begins with the proclamation of Immanuel — a God who is *with us*. Our need for both the presence of God and for the presence of others only grows as the New Testament continues to reveal God's story.

After Christ's commandment to "go and make disciples of all nations" (Matthew 28), He ascends to heaven. The Book of Acts begins with that moment, and then transitions quickly into the events surrounding the coming of the Holy Spirit. After the dust settles, we're given a clear picture of how followers of Jesus begin to live in response to all that's happened before their eyes...

"And they devoted themselves to the apostles' teaching and
the fellowship, to the breaking of bread and the prayers.
And awe came upon every soul, and many wonders and
signs were being done through the apostles. And all who
believed were together and had all things in common.
And they were selling their possessions and belongings and
distributing the proceeds to all, as any had need. And day
by day, attending the temple together and breaking bread
in their homes, they received their food with glad and
generous hearts, praising God and having favor with all
the people. And the Lord added to their number day by
day those who were being saved."

Acts 2:42-47

It's easy to sense the momentum that's building in this early Christian community, and to feel the joy of everything they're experiencing with each other.

They're learning about the life of Jesus together, celebrating the Lord's Supper together, and praying together. The community is filled with awe whenever they get out of the way and watch God show up. They view their possessions as objects on loan from God, and their spirit of generosity compels them to willingly give away any object as the need presents itself. They keep meeting together every day in the temple courts and in their homes, and they do so with hearts that are full of gladness and sincerity. If anyone wants to know what it looks like when followers of Jesus adopt a Posture of Community, this is it.

But we're not only given a *model* of community to follow. God also gives us a *mandate*.

The Mandate of Community

We follow Jesus *for* ourselves, but not *by* ourselves, and the verses below from the Book of Hebrews illustrate this concept.

> *"And let us consider how to stir up one another to love and good works, not neglecting to meet together, as is the habit of some, but encouraging one another, and all the more as you see the Day drawing near."*

Hebrews 10:24-25

Meeting regularly with those in our Christian communities will help us grow into all that God has for us, and that growth trajectory is the hallmark of The 3:30 Life. We'll not only become the recipients of this Life, but we'll also become the agents of it for others. This Life simply cannot be experienced in isolation with a bent toward individualism, but must be experienced intentionally with a Posture toward Community — a community where we encourage each other to live every day for That Day.

This only becomes clearer when we turn the page into Hebrews 11. Commonly called "The Hall of Faith," we're given several real-life inspirational examples of people who have walked by faith, and who can help us discover the essence of what it means to do the same. It's an amazing and essential read, and worth your time to take a break and read it now. In a very real sense, these men and women also become our Community, as evidenced at the beginning of the following chapter:

"Therefore, since we are surrounded by so great a cloud
of witnesses, let us also lay aside every weight, and sin
which clings so closely, and let us run with endurance the
race that is set before us, looking to Jesus, the founder and
perfecter of our faith, who for the joy that was set before
him endured the cross, despising the shame, and is seated
at the right hand of the throne of God."

Hebrews 12:1-2

When we live with an awareness of this great cloud of witnesses — with the recognition that we stand alongside the faith heroes who have come before us — we learn to recognize that we're a part of something bigger than ourselves. What began as a mandate to "not give up meeting together" becomes illustrated with real-life examples who are cheering us on as we run the race God has given us — a race that begins and ends with Jesus, for His glory alone.

This is what happens when we embrace a Posture of Community.

> Even though there may be times in our lives when we're removed from people, isolation should never become the Posture we choose.

CONCLUSION

We all remember the worldwide Pandemic that began in early 2020 — a season we've never been through before. What we knew in our heads in 2019 became something we felt in the core of our beings in 2020. Our need for community was made painfully clear when the ability to gather was taken away. Our need to avoid isolation moved from our heads to our hearts, as we began to feel the truth that The Following was never meant to be a go-it-alone proposition. Even though there may be times in our lives when we're removed from people, isolation should never become the posture we choose. If there's an opportunity to be with others regularly, we'd be hard-pressed to make a case that it's not what's best for us, or for them. In the meals we share, in the groups and retreats we attend, in our Sunday worship gatherings and our Monday coffee conversations, these are the places and spaces where we receive courage, strength, accountability, and hope.

These are the huddles we long for.

In the days and weeks ahead, be on the lookout for those moments when you're in this type of community, and the moments when you're not. Introverts and extroverts alike — push yourself into a greater awareness of what happens in these moments of community that can't happen when you're alone.

Because these Postures are all about preparation and potential, then the things you'll discover in community will prepare you to live The 3:30 Life, unleashing the potential of Christ's life in you, and through you.

We were created for this.

You were created for this.

CHAPTER 20

Service

START HERE

SCAN TO WATCH

Living By *DESIGN* Rather Than Default

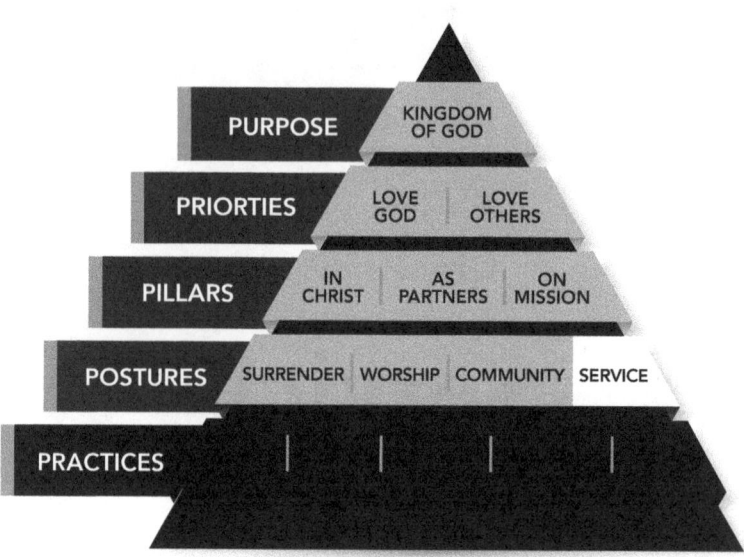

I retired from the NFL in May 2001, and it wasn't too long after that Lori and I felt God's call to full-time ministry serving the student-athletes back at Stanford University. Having both been athletes there ourselves, we really connected with the young men and women on campus and loved gathering with them as often as possible and teaching them about what it means to know and follow Jesus.

Within the first couple years, however, we realized a piece seemed to be missing in our efforts to convey the depth of who Jesus truly is. We would meet and study God's Word often and did our best to answer their continual questions about a life of faith. Yet something appeared to be falling short when it came to connecting their head-knowledge with the passion of their hearts. Lori and I soon realized that we needed an outlet to help them put their faith in action, so we began to dream about getting our students out into the world to serve others. Our first thought was to find a long weekend where we could take a group of students down to Mexico to build homes in the marginalized communities there. If you're familiar with college athletics (or honestly any age of athletics lately), you can appreciate the impossibility of finding an open weekend without practice or games to take a group of student-athletes away from campus.

The aha moment came one day while studying Scripture, and we thought deeper about the fact that there were plenty of "neighbors" to love within minutes of us, just beyond the borders of the Stanford campus. As we continued to press into this invitation from God, we were privileged to meet a beautiful elderly woman named Dorothy. Dorothy had been widowed at a very young age, and with God's help had successfully raised four children on her own while at the same time becoming a spiritual pillar in the East Palo Alto community. At the time when we met her, Dorothy had just recently lost both of her legs due to complications from diabetes. After visiting Dorothy in her home, we quickly offered to gather a group of the student-athletes and come to her house over a weekend as soon as possible to do anything we could to help make her life "a little better." Given the limited resources we had, we offered to clean her windows, provide some lawn care, declutter and deep clean her house. If this is where the story ended, it would have been enough for us.

But before that weekend arrived, we discovered God's plans for this endeavor to be bigger than we could have ever dreamed.

After that initial meeting with Dorothy and having our hearts engaged in ways we hadn't experienced before, we resolved to do whatever we could to help her. That involved telling anyone and everyone we knew about Dorothy's situation and inviting them to join us in the efforts as well. Through a series of God-appointed introductions, I found myself meeting with a highly successful business leader in our community, and that's when things got interesting.

He and I sat down for a coffee meeting one morning and he allowed me to share the vision of what we hoped to do with a group of students for Dorothy. When I finished he shook his head and said, "Steve, there's a Habitat for Humanity on the way to my office, and lately when I've been driving past it, I've felt a tug on my heart to get involved in helping more people with some of what the Lord has blessed me with. Tell me what you truly dream of doing for this woman and let's see what we might be able to accomplish."

I told him about how being in a wheelchair presented Dorothy with new challenges to even get around her home, much less enjoy it. We needed to widen doorways, install ramps, make her kitchen and bathrooms functional for her, and allow her to still get outside on her own to enjoy her yard, especially her treasured vegetable gardens which she had planted each and every year of her life. We praise God for orchestrating that meeting and the continued financial support that flowed out of his generous heart. In the end, we were able to accomplish an enormous project for Dorothy that resembled something akin to the Extreme Makeover Home Edition show (if you ever had the privilege to watch that back in the early 2000s). Several hundred people soon gathered over a weekend and we ended up completely recreating her home — and all of our lives were changed for the better in the process. Years later, I still tell people of the time when "we just brought our loaves and fish together," and the Lord did a miracle through His people.

But that's not where this heart-warming story ends.

The single project at Dorothy's house grew into quarterly service weekends where we'd invite the students on campus, as well as those in our local community, to serve our "neighbors." Thousands upon thousands of people participated in these service projects over the years. The project for Dorothy led us to bigger and bigger projects. We were able to rebuild a home that served single teenage mothers, improve the facilities of a myriad of local ministries, and make over all seven of the public schools in East Palo Alto that lacked adequate resources to serve their children so they could learn, thrive, and look forward to attending school each day. Churches in the area began to take notice and either decided to work in partnership with our ministry, or take our model and implement it with their own vision, in their own ways to do similar good works in the community. Who could have ever imagined how a single act of service for Dorothy could turn into this? God did. He took our loaves and our fish, and multiplied them for the good of His people. Time and time again.

We learned so much during those years. We learned that a life of service becomes contagious because our souls were created to serve others; the joy and inspiration that came into countless people's lives through these projects are still having ripple effects to this day. We learned that progress can happen fast, and that it doesn't have to take years of planning and red tape before the first shovel hits the ground. We learned that a posture of service is actually the most fulfilling way to live, because it's already hardwired into the DNA of our souls. However, the most important thing we learned was loud and clear, bold and challenging, and worthy of a complete perspective overhaul...

**We learned that we're the most like Christ when
we're loving and serving people in His name.**

If the third Posture of Community is where we recognize our need *for* others, then this fourth Posture of Service is where we recognize the needs *of* others — and then do something about it.

THE ESSENCE OF CHRIST

When Scripture gives us glimpses into the heart of Jesus, what we discover always includes a posture of serving others. It's not only something Jesus *does*, but it's who He *is*. The following words reveal His essence as a humble servant in rich and powerful ways:

> *"So if there is any encouragement in Christ, any comfort*
> *from love, any participation in the Spirit, any affection*
> *and sympathy, complete my joy by being of the same mind,*
> *having the same love, being in full accord and of one mind.*
> *Do nothing from selfish ambition or conceit, but in humility*
> *count others more significant than yourselves. Let each of*
> *you look not only to his own interests, but also to the interests*
> *of others. Have this mind among yourselves, which is yours*
> *in Christ Jesus, who, though he was in the form of God,*
> *did not count equality with God a thing to be grasped, but*
> *emptied himself, by taking the form of a servant, being born*
> *in the likeness of men. And being found in human form, he*
> *humbled himself by becoming obedient to the point of death,*
> *even death on a cross. Therefore God has highly exalted him*
> *and bestowed on him the name that is above every name, so*
> *that at the name of Jesus every knee should bow, in heaven*
> *and on earth and under the earth, and every tongue confess*
> *that Jesus Christ is Lord, to the glory of God the Father."*

Philippians 2:1-11

Jesus is God, but He didn't view that as something to hold onto. Rather, He willingly surrendered His authority and made Himself just like us.

In doing so, He embodied the real-life example of what it means to be a faithful servant, becoming the King who willingly forfeited everything that's rightfully His, all for the benefit of others. And He did it in a spirit of humility.

In Matthew 25, Jesus puts words to a future event that will be centered around the importance of serving other people, and the reality of Who we're really serving in the process:

> *"When the Son of Man comes in his glory, and all the angels*
> *with him, then he will sit on his glorious throne. Before him*
> *will be gathered all the nations, and he will separate people one*
> *from another as a shepherd separates the sheep from the goats.*
> *And he will place the sheep on his right, but the goats on the*
> *left. Then the King will say to those on his right, 'Come, you*
> *who are blessed by my Father, inherit the kingdom prepared*
> *for you from the foundation of the world. For I was hungry*
> *and you gave me food, I was thirsty and you gave me drink,*
> *I was a stranger and you welcomed me, I was naked and you*
> *clothed me, I was sick and you visited me, I was in prison and*
> *you came to me.' Then the righteous will answer him, saying,*
> *'Lord, when did we see you hungry and feed you, or thirsty*
> *and give you drink? And when did we see you a stranger and*
> *welcome you, or naked and clothe you? And when did we see*
> *you sick or in prison and visit you?' And the King will answer*
> *them, 'Truly, I say to you, as you did it to one of the least of*
> *these my brothers, you did it to me.'"*

Matthew 25:31-40

> The Posture of Service is of monumental importance to Jesus, and if we miss it, we'll actually miss the purpose for which we were designed.

The story goes on to describe those who saw the same people in need, but who didn't raise a finger to help them. Jesus doesn't mince His words at all, saying our lack of service toward others equates to a lack of service toward Him personally, and we don't belong in His presence.

The Posture of Service is of monumental importance to Jesus, and if we miss it, we'll actually miss the purpose for which we were designed. He's saying that we can't possibly have *not* served others in those situations if we really knew Him. Serving the needs of "the least of these" is the natural outgrowth of being in Christ. As we simply say "yes" to every next step, we experience the beautiful life we've been created for — a life that's intertwined and strengthened in the service of others. Because when we stare into their eyes, it's Jesus staring back.

What Does a Posture of Service Look Like?

The businessman who became our main resource for our Stanford ministry gave me a devotional book. It's called "My Utmost For His Highest" by Oswald Chambers, and outside of reading Scripture every day, no book has spoken into my life more consistently and with greater clarity than this daily devotional. I can count on one hand the number of days I've missed reading it since then. Listen to how Chambers defines service:

*"Service is the overflow which pours from a life filled with love and devotion.
But strictly speaking, there is no call to that. Service is what I bring
to the relationship and is the reflection of my identification with the
nature of God. Service becomes a natural part of my life. God brings
me into the proper relationship with Himself so that I can understand
His call, and then I serve Him on my own out of a motivation of
absolute love. Service to God is the deliberate love-gift of a nature that
has heard the call of God. Service is an expression of my nature, and
God's call is an expression of His nature. Therefore, when I receive His
nature and hear His call, His divine voice resounds throughout His
nature and mine and the two become one in service. The Son of God
reveals Himself in me, and out of devotion to Him service becomes my
everyday way of life."*

Even though serving others becomes a practice in our lives, it's far more significant as a Posture we lean into. The Posture of Service involves an awareness — a growing sensitivity to the Spirit that calls us to participate in the story of anyone God places in our path. We don't need to take inventory of our own capacities or perceived limitations. Rather, we just need to go and be present, and in the midst of being present, God shows us what to do next. These are the times when our unique passions and abilities intersect with His unique provisions, and the loaves and fish we bring to the table are exponentially multiplied. It's in these moments when we see the Increase of Jesus most clearly, because it's then we're most clearly living The 3:30 Life.

A WORD OF WARNING

As you might imagine, anything that directly connects us with Jesus will become a prime target of attack for the enemy. He'll tempt us in two main areas.

The Pride of Humility — When we posture ourselves toward serving others, we're admitting that we're not the heroes of the story, but the enemy wants us to believe something different. He wants us to take our acts of service, and through some act of veiled humility, broadcast our serving stories to anyone who might be listening. On the surface, we appear humble, but we're actually doing it for the applause of people. When we do so, we focus the story back on Me rather than He. In the prayers we pray, the stories we tell, the names we drop, and the posts we make on social media, we can easily succumb to taking immense pride in our own false humility. The ultimate question we must answer is this: Who are we trying to point people toward in talking about our service?

> These are the times when our unique passions and abilities intersect with His unique provisions, and the loaves and fish we bring to the table are exponentially multiplied.

The Trap of Excuses — When it comes to serving, we're quite skilled at coming up with a myriad of reasons to cross over to the other side of the road, and to just keep walking (Luke 10:31-32). Many people self-talk their way out of any serving opportunity that God places in front of them, often citing a perceived lack of resources, a fear of some unintended outcome, or a lack of preparation. But my contention here is that service is not primarily an action, but rather a posture of readiness and awareness that unleashes us in the moment — in *any* moment. We like to make plans because they're more formulaic, but being prepared to serve others when God prompts us ought to be instinctual, not formulaic. Living by design requires positioning ourselves for service long before we enter into any specific event. It's messy, less defined, and with fewer boundaries, but it's the only way to live for anyone desiring to experience The 3:30 Life. As I've heard it said, "My yes is already on the table, and I'm just waiting for the invitation."

CONCLUSION

Are you ready to experience God being God? We hear the stories from Scripture and from others, and we're inspired from the outside, but a Posture of Service allows *you* to become part of the story. Are you ready to come alive through service in ways that nothing else replicates? There's a deep transaction of the soul that takes place when we serve people. We see Jesus from the front row. We overcome the divisions of the enemy. We look past all the stuff that pride invites us to fixate on, and we humbly embrace *all* of humanity.

So really lean into this with readiness and anticipation. Recognize the temptation we feel to be elevated, and choose instead to be connected on the ground, to the Savior. Learn to serve everyone, allowing it to become habitual and reflexive in the lives of your family, friends, neighbors, and strangers. Guard carefully against what you'll get out of it, if a person deserves it or not, or whether or not you'll be paid back. Lean into a trust of God's abundant resources, and set aside any mindset of scarcity and impossibility. Let love become your sole motivator, because HE first loved you (1 John 4:19).

This is where you say "yes" to every next step.

This is where God gives you the best opportunities of your entire life.

This is where the Increase of Jesus is unleashed.

So what are you waiting for?

CHAPTER 21

Practices

START HERE

SCAN TO WATCH

Living By *DESIGN* Rather Than Default

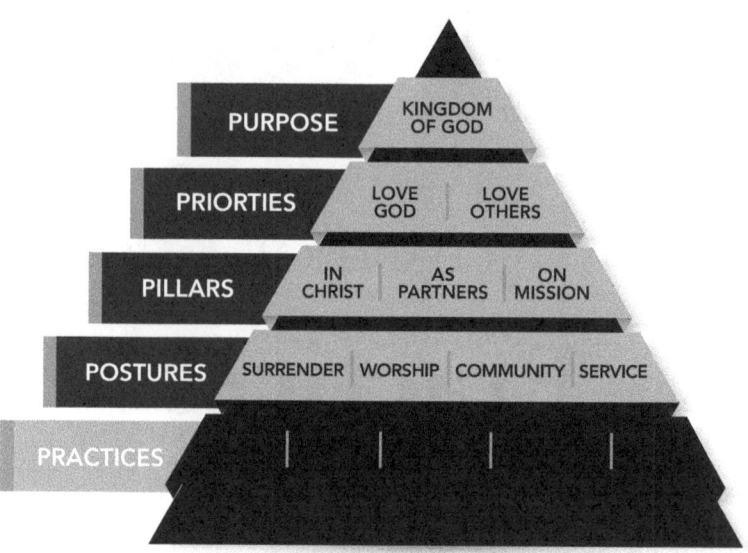

Though there might be some debate on who first coined the phrase "West Coast Offense," most attribute it to Bill Parcells, and it most certainly refers to the offensive system devised by Coach Walsh. After I retired from the NFL and was living back in the Bay Area, Coach had an office in the Stanford athletic department. I was on campus most days meeting with students and would often stop by to talk to him. On one such occasion, I asked what he thought about the "West Coast Offense" label, since it clearly stuck and wasn't going anywhere.

Steve: Do you not like it?

Coach: It doesn't matter. We just had our offense. I didn't give it any label.

Steve: Well, because it's so thrown around now...

Coach: Yeah. Now it's just thrown around everywhere.

Steve: But it pertains to what you guys were doing?

Coach: It pertains basically to *how we taught* and what *mechanics we taught*, more than the plays. And *how we practiced*, more than the plays.

I love it when we get a glimpse into the perspective of the author!

A simple online search of the West Coast Offense will tell you, "The offense is characterized by short, horizontal passing routes in lieu of running plays to 'stretch out' defenses, opening up the potential for long runs or long passes."

The author will tell you the truth, and the truth according to Coach Walsh was that what happened on the *practice field* is what made all the difference.

Search engines and other outsiders want to talk about the *outcomes* and the *plays*. The author would tell you it was about the *process*, and how the offense was *taught* and *practiced*.

What happens on the practice field matters, and this example easily translates to the biblical idea of walking. When we follow Jesus, we "walk" together with Him, and this walking reveals that we're truly in Christ: "Whoever says he abides in him ought to walk in the same way in which he walked" (1 John 2:6). Is our walk perfect every time? Of course not. Sometimes when we walk we also stumble, we fall, and we limp. God knows, and we must always know, that it's about *progress* over *perfection*, and about the *journey* over the *destination*. When we walk as Jesus walked, and when we go where Jesus leads, we'll witness Him pour His resources into those spaces as He sees fit. And it's those experiences that inspire us to practice as much as possible.

WHAT ARE PRACTICES?

When we think about practicing, our minds immediately jump to the athletic stadium, an indoor training facility, or to a track, swimming pool, golf course, etc. But practicing extends well beyond our athletic pursuits and arenas. It can extend into our living rooms where we practice piano or other instruments, and in our kitchens where we learn to balance nutrition and prepare meals for friends and family. It happens in studios or on a canvas as we apply ourselves in the arts, and in our garages where we might learn to restore an antiquated automobile. You get the idea. Whatever their shape and form, we intuitively understand our arenas of practicing.

**Practices are the spaces in which we identify
and apply the correct information, time and time
again, because the "game" is coming.**

Our practice fields are where we *apply* the truth of everything God's inviting us into. They're where we show up and do the work to grow and progress. We may be near a coach or a mentor, or we may be alone with only the Spirit of God. When we engage in practices, we're committing to a window of time during which the many detours and distractions of life are strategically pushed into the periphery.

As Coach Walsh taught me, every practice is intentionally designed and scripted. So if that's the case, then what happens on the practice field must logically become a collection of movements called "drills." In the Christian life, drills are synonymous with disciplines, habits, and routines — and we all inherently know that these things are valuable for anything we set out to accomplish. In the upcoming pages I'll present the five core Practices of The 3:30 Life, but they'll be rehearsed over and over again through the *drills* that we commit to. These drills are designed to help us walk as Jesus walked.

AN UNEXPECTED PICTURE

One day I drove by an enormous children's bounce house, and if you're a parent, you know the kind. There it was in all its glory, in the middle of a family's front yard, just inviting the young and the young-at-heart into its netted walls. Obviously, the family had selected this precise bounce house based on a picture of it they saw beforehand, long before it was ever fully inflated on their front lawn for their children to enjoy, and for me to drive past.

The Four Postures, as discussed in the previous chapters, point us to the picture of what The 3:30 Life looks like (similar to the bounce house) when it's fully inflated. The Practices we discuss next are what will "inflate" the Postures to take the form they are designed for. These Practices will unlock our potential as we engage in a variety of drills, disciplines, and routines that will help us along the way. They'll begin as conscious efforts on our part, but they won't stay that way because in time, with repetition, they will become instinctual. In athletics, performance must become subconscious in order to be ready for the pace and pressure of a real game. The Postures of Surrender, Worship, Community and Service are like that. With repetition, they'll begin to emanate from a life that's continually being molded and transformed on the practice fields of Pausing, Praying, Learning, Gathering, and Giving.

To ensure we don't drift away from a grace-based approach to following Jesus, we must always remember...

It's all about progress over perfection, and about the journey over the destination.

WHAT WILL PRACTICES DO?

Practices change us, shape us, and lead to personal transformation. Practices are where we learn to seek first the Kingdom of God. They are where we prioritize our relationship with Jesus, and help establish it so that everything else in our lives finds its rightful place within that hierarchy. They reinforce the paradigms of abiding in Christ as partners on mission. Ultimately, these Practices bolster everything above them on The 3:30 Life Pyramid, keeping us on track as we follow Jesus, and ensuring we continue growing as His disciples.

You may have guessed by now, but I'm not a fan of Christian formulas because they tend to promise a specific outcome that only God can ultimately create. However, in the area of the Practices that lead to personal transformation, there *actually is* a formula I endorse. It's something that I, and others, have utilized for years and it's something that's worthy of a conversation here. The formula is this:

(Information + Application) x Repetition = Transformation

In other words, *when we apply the correct information over and over and over, we'll experience the personal transformation that God has designed for us.* Let's explore each component further.

INFORMATION — We live in the information age, and we all consume it every day. There's a giant ocean of information available to us, and while most of it isn't harmful, that doesn't mean it's beneficial either. For example, we've all had the experience of performing an internet search, and after an hour, we can't remember where we started, or how we got to where we are. This type of mindless information consumption is a trap, and exemplifies the importance of identifying relevant information. This will feel countercultural, because it requires us to look past what we default to, and into the design model given to us from our Creator.

APPLICATION — Consuming the correct information is the first step, but then we must take the next step and apply that information in our daily life. Much like a bottle of sunscreen in the container, it needs to be applied onto our skin to work. It's this application of the right information that God desires for us. It will require discernment to determine when and how to apply what we know in our daily lives, and this is the essence of wisdom.

REPETITION — At the most basic level, repetition is repeating something. By doing something again and again, we discover what's working and what isn't. We can make tweaks and adjustments when we repeat the same action, and this allows us to iterate until we eventually get it right. We try new things, we learn the correct things, and we gain clarity about all things.

TRANSFORMATION — As we're engaged in applying the correct information time and time again, we experience authentic and lasting transformation by the power of the Spirit. Our hearts become more aligned with the heart of God, and we begin to walk in the manner of Jesus.

> Our hearts become more aligned with the heart of God, and we begin to walk in the manner of Jesus.

But first, a word of warning that applies to everyone, myself included. Ask any athlete, and they'll tell you that some days on the practice field are inspiring, and full of joy and measurable growth. But other days — many days — will feel like a grind, and will appear mundane without any immediate measurable progress. No matter what practicing *feels* like, all athletes must learn the value of making repeated "deposits" they'll withdraw at a future date.

The same is true of those who follow Jesus. We'll have rewarding, invigorating, and fulfilling days where we know we're growing spiritually closer to Him, but we'll also have days that feel mundane and difficult where we don't perceive any growth at all.

The ancient Greeks had two words for "time" — chronos and kairos. "Chronos" time is how we live every day. It's sequential and where we derive the word "chronological." However, "kairos" time is something that exists outside of our day-to-day lives, and points us to some unique or opportune moment in time. Practices teach us to trust God in the chronos, because our hearts long for the kairos. We push into every *Today* with design and purpose on the practice field, because our souls await the complete and unimaginably great victory of *That Day*.

CONCLUSION

As I've mentioned before, the Five Practices that lead us into personal transformation are: Pausing, Praying, Learning, Gathering, and Giving. We show up to *those* practice fields regularly, and the "ing" ending of each indicates the reality of something that's ongoing and continuous. In the next five chapters, you'll dig deeper into each of these Practices, and you'll become equipped to identify and apply the correct information, and to do that over and over again.

But, before you close the pages of this chapter, I invite you to imagine your potential future. Dream about what it might look like for you to become a more pausing, more praying, more learning, more gathering, and more giving person. Envision what your life might become if you learn to slow down, to talk to God, to be well-studied, to value all people, and to be generous. Imagine this becoming true of you on the outside, because you're experiencing real transformation on the inside.

So may you awaken to this new quality of Life — this quality of *abundant* Life.

And may you know that this truly is the Life you've been waiting for all along.

CHAPTER 22

Pausing

START HERE

SCAN TO WATCH

Living By *DESIGN* Rather Than Default

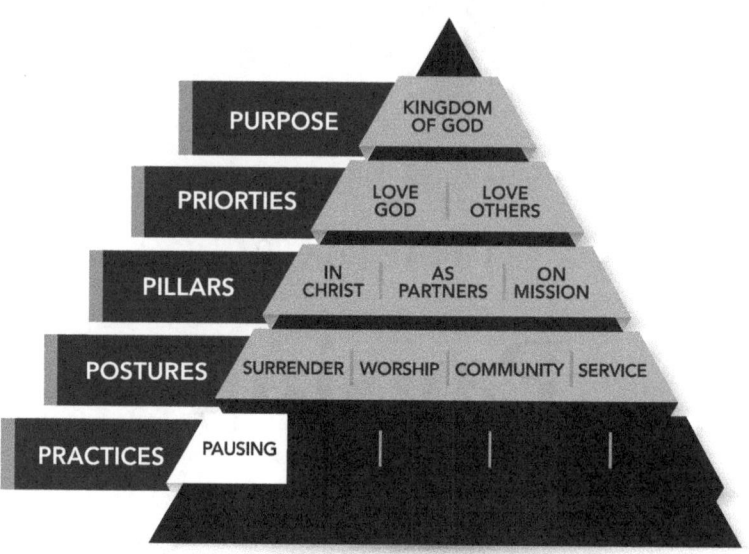

Ask any quarterback at any level of the game, and they'll tell you that their *ability* to avoid the rush is a primary factor in their success. Conversely, they'll also tell you that their *inability* to avoid the rush is a primary indicator in a defeat. Their personal effectiveness, their follow-through, and even their physical well-being are all at stake when "the rush" is a factor. The opposing team's defensive coordinator will spend an entire week implementing a strategy that's designed to disrupt the offense. Every one of those strategies will inevitably be crafted to produce both worry and hurry in the life of the QB. If you're a fan of the game, you already know what it looks like when a QB *can* avoid the rush, and when he *can't*. That's why the space of the practice field is so important, and it's why quarterbacks practice drills that are specifically designed to help them learn to avoid and handle the rush during the game.

In the same way, we intuitively understand what it means to rush our way through life. Whether it's the never-ending deadlines we're under, the frustration of rush-hour traffic, or the pressure to respond to our emails and complete our to-do lists, we have learned to live in a constant state of busyness. At best, we're aware of it, and we know it's not ideal. At worst, we're unaware, and even sometimes equate our busy pace with our personal success.

That being said, as we consider the Five Practices of The 3:30 Life, this is why the Practice of Pausing is the perfect place to start. Even though these Practices will overlap and intersect, Pausing is foundational to all the others. If the game really is coming, then Pausing becomes a critical space where The 3:30 Life is unlocked.

I remember when I first learned about the transformation of a caterpillar into a butterfly. In order for that unique metamorphosis to take place, the caterpillar must enter the cocoon. What happens in the cocoon is nothing short of miraculous. In that quiet and peaceful place, the beauty that was always within the DNA of the caterpillar is unlocked, and the transformation is magnificent.

Transformation occurs as we learn to avoid the rush of life.

> Branches abide. They remain grafted into the life
> of the vine, and they don't fight against it.

PAUSING AND ABIDING

If you asked me what single biblical passage best describes the Practice of Pausing, I'd point you to the "vine and the branches" illustration in John 15. We've discussed this important passage already in Chapter 13 when we talked about the Three Pillars, but we need to push beyond that.

Jesus speaking...

> *"I am the true vine, and my Father is the vinedresser. Every branch in me that does not bear fruit he takes away, and every branch that does bear fruit he prunes, that it may bear more fruit. Already you are clean because of the word that I have spoken to you. Abide in me, and I in you. As the branch cannot bear fruit by itself, unless it abides in the vine, neither can you, unless you abide in me. I am the vine; you are the branches. Whoever abides in me and I in him, he it is that bears much fruit, for apart from me you can do nothing."*

John 15:1-5

As you reflect on that passage, do you see where the life of the branch is found? Can you identify the function of the branch, and the function of the vine? Do you take notice of what the branch is designed *to do*, and what it's designed *to be*?

Branches abide. They remain grafted into the life of the vine, and they don't fight against it. The branches don't work harder to become the best branches they can be. Their connectivity to the vine is of vital importance because that's what will produce the fruit the Vinedresser intends. Every branch knows that, at the end of the day, there is no fruit they can produce on their own. Vines produce the fruit that the branches bear.

We are branches. We are not vines, and we are most certainly not the Vinedresser. And we discover this reality deeply and acutely when we engage in the Practice of Pausing. It's precisely *this* rhythm of pausing and abiding that will inform our lives and our decisions, and will serve to refine our already-too-busy schedules as we follow Jesus wherever He leads.

> Pausing is where we become deeply aware of His presence *with* us, His voice *to* us, and His sovereignty *over* us.

PAUSING AND BEING STILL

In addition to the vine and the branches, a well-known passage in Psalm 46 serves to illustrate the priority of Pausing:

> *"God is our refuge and strength,*
> *a very present help in trouble.*
> *Therefore we will not fear though the earth gives way,*
> *though the mountains be moved into the heart of the sea,*
> *though its waters roar and foam,*
> *though the mountains tremble at its swelling.*
> Selah

> *"'Be still, and know that I am God.*
> *I will be exalted among the nations,*
> *I will be exaslted in the earth!'*
> *The Lord of hosts is with us;*
> *the God of Jacob is our fortress."*
> Selah

Psalm 46:1-3, 10-11

The scenario described here is full of chaos and uncertainty. When everything outside of our control seems to be crumbling down around us — when the hurries and worries of life crescendo and roar — God says to "be still, and know that I am God." Much like a QB trying to avoid the rush, God isn't trying to disconnect us from our circumstances, nor encourage us to deny their existence. Rather, when we show up to the Pause, we see what we're supposed to see, and we know that He is God. We're reminded, restored, and refreshed. We see our lives more clearly, because we see them in the light of who He is, not in the light of who we are. While there's no perfect English word that captures its meaning, scholars tend to think that "Selah" likely means to "pause" or to "stop and listen." Psalm 46 reminds us that in the Pause, we experience *calm* in the midst of the chaos, we're offered *confidence* in the Creator of all things, and we become acutely aware of the absolute *certainty* in the outcome.

THE PRACTICE OF PAUSING

So what is the Practice of Pausing? What does it look like, and how can it best be expressed? The following definition provides a good anchor point:

> **Pausing is an intentional space where we slow down**
> **so we can see things from God's perspective and**
> **mitigate against the worries and hurries of life.**

Pausing removes us from the hurry and worry of our normal lives. It's where we avoid the rush, and where we enter the cocoon. It's where we connect with the Vine — where we are still, and where we intimately discover Him as God. Most of the time it's done alone, but there are some occasions when it's done with others. The Pause recalibrates us toward our true God-given design, so that a life of He rather than Me is unleashed.

But let's face it: The Practice of Pausing is incredibly counterintuitive. For many people, it just doesn't add up or even feel possible. We constantly seem driven to work harder, longer, and faster. Our ambitions carry us toward the urgent things, and then push those urgent demands to the top of our to-do lists.

But pausing teaches us the difference between the urgent and the important.

In pausing, we create space where the Creator can meet with us on His terms.

In the Pause, we learn that when we go *slower*, we end up going *farther*. Because The 3:30 Life involves an expectant hope in the heavenly multiplier that only God can supply, we get excited about Pausing opportunities because that's where He shows up. Pausing is where we become deeply aware of His presence *with* us, His voice *to* us, and His sovereignty *over* us. Due to our finite amount of time and capacity, when we refuse to retain some margin for the Practice of Pausing, we'll miss out on where God is going, and what we're being invited into. Pausing teaches us that our "no" to the urgent strengthens our "yes" to the important, and where we learn to recognize the truly essential things of life.

DRILLS AND DISCIPLINES

As I write this book, my son Blake is a quarterback at the collegiate level, but his football journey started a long time ago. Blake and I have been practicing together for as long as I can remember. Developing the postures every QB needs to be prepared and to unlock their potential has been my focus with Blake from the beginning. While the drills and disciplines have morphed and evolved as he's grown and improved, the focus of our practice together has always been the same

— to "inflate" the postures he will need to be successful when the game comes. These days, I mostly watch Blake practice and play, and it brings a smile to my face every time as I see him continuing to grow and progress. The key, however, is to never quit practicing because we can never rest on our laurels. While the drills and disciplines may adjust over time, they will remain mission-critical as long as Blake wants to play the position.

For as long as we live, practice is vital, and that's why drills and disciplines are so important.

When we look at the disciplines of Pausing throughout Christian history, they've been described as quiet times, retreats, moments of silence, solitude, and the like. Saints throughout the ages have shown us how important these habits are, and they've served me personally throughout my life as a Christ follower. I've also found that, in following Jesus over the years, those timeless disciplines don't constitute an exhaustive list, and that there are other ways to practice Pausing in our lives. For example:

- Turning off our devices when we get into the car, and using those moments to pray and ponder.

- Taking a walk during our workdays.

- Finding a tree and sitting under it for a bit.

- Closing our eyes and feeling the breeze blow across our face.

- Going outside just before bed and sitting quietly in the dark.

- Getting lost in the stars, and in the grandeur of the world around us, discovering the beauty of knowing that He is God.

- Taking a walk in our neighborhood after dinner.

- Using a journal to capture what's being revealed to us in the pause.

- Getting away for an extended period of time by spending the better part of a day in nature.

These are just a few examples. I encourage you to do what works best for you, and be both creative and contemplative as you do so.

CONCLUSION

So what now? For those who are already involved in the Practice of Pausing, then keep going, but add one more discipline or drill. The more we experiment with the habits associated with Pausing, the stronger we'll become and the more we'll learn to fight for these spaces in our everyday lives.

For those who haven't yet embraced Pausing, pick one or two habits and try them today. At some point, everyone who wants to get in shape needs to pick up the bar and start lifting regardless of how much weight you can put on the ends. Think of someone whose walk with Jesus you admire. Get this list in front of them, and ask them to help you learn how. If you see Jesus in them, then they've obviously practiced Pausing, and they'll have an abundance of wisdom to share.

Finally, don't be afraid to lean into the habits that make your heart come alive with the things of God, and then to create the needed margin to experience Him daily.

This is where you'll most discover the beauty of pondering, preparing, and prioritizing. This is where you'll learn to stand against the general inertia of life that pushes us in a direction where other people dictate our every next move.

So show up.

Avoid the rush.

Enter the cocoon.

Abide.

Be still.

Know that He is God.

And be transformed.

CHAPTER 23

Praying

START HERE

SCAN TO WATCH

Living By *DESIGN* Rather Than Default

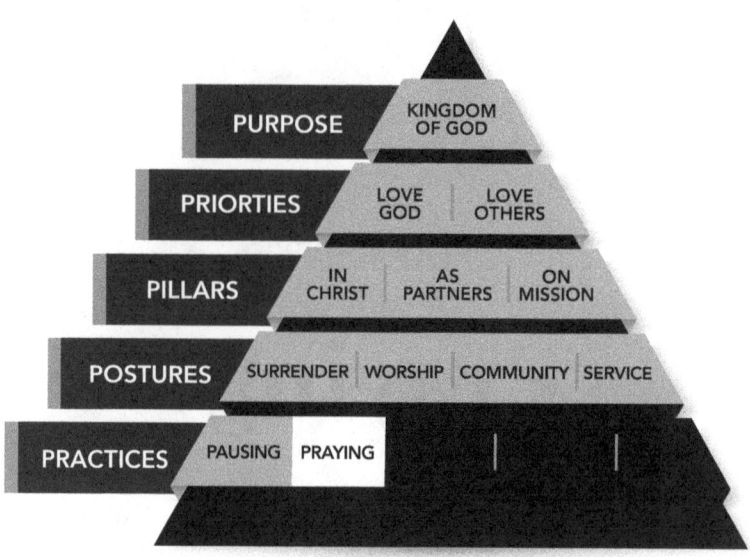

Have you ever been watching a football game and seen the quarterback walk to the sideline, pick up a phone, and start talking to someone on the other end? Have you ever wondered who he's talking to, or what they're talking about? I actually get asked about that all the time. When it happens in a game situation, the quarterback is communicating with the offensive coordinator or the QB coach up "in the booth." Even though the phone has been replaced by the headset in recent years, this communication is vitally important, because the coach is seeing things from an elevated vantage point that allows him to assess the big picture. The quarterback must acknowledge his own limited perspective, while also embracing the insights from his coach who has a superior view of the action. The quarterback needs to know what the coach sees. In my playing days, *that* conversation provided me the space to pause, to get my uncertainties addressed, and to have new real-time insights revealed. I was always better in the game after I talked with the coach.

Sounds a lot like prayer, doesn't it? Praying reflects a strong conviction that we're always better when we speak to and hear from God, who has a higher vantage point than us and who designed it all in the first place. As we willingly acknowledge our own limited perspective, the Practice of Praying equips us, reveals new insights to us, and ultimately transforms us.

Our Access to The Father

The writer of the Book of Hebrews paints a beautiful picture of what Christ's death and resurrection have accomplished.

> *"Since then we have a great high priest who has passed through the heavens, Jesus, the Son of God, let us hold fast our confession. For we do not have a high priest who is unable to sympathize with our weaknesses, but one who in every respect has been tempted as we are, yet without sin. Let us then with confidence draw near to the throne of grace, that we may receive mercy and find grace to help in time of need."*

Hebrews 4:14-16

All throughout the Old Testament, the nation of Israel established a lifestyle rhythm around the High Priest. He would enact the rituals of atonement, and would do so through a detailed system of animal sacrifices. At the center of his role, the High Priest was the person who stood as a mediator between God and man. The people would bring sacrifices to him and he would offer them before God on their behalf. The people's sins would be covered but only temporarily, and this would repeat itself year after year.

So when Jesus is called "the Great High Priest," this backstory establishes the foundation for a new reality. We now have a High Priest who went through everything we'll go through, yet who was without sin. Jesus is the once-for-all Mediator between God and man, and His death is a process that never needs to be repeated again. As a result, those who are in Christ (Pillar #1) have restored access to the Father through Him, and that access allows us to approach the throne of God *with confidence*.

The Practice of Praying stands on the foundation of *that* reality.

It's a reality that goes far beyond a reconciliation of God's heavenly ledger, although it involves that as well. It invites us to celebrate the fact that the heart of God desires deep communion and relationship with us, and the price Jesus paid to bring us back into this relationship must always serve as an indication of how important we are to Him. Embracing this reality creates great freedom to come to God, and to bring our hopes and expectations into His presence as often as possible. As we pray, we embrace the tension between revering God and having confidence in Him, between His holiness and our accessibility, and between our fear and His approachability. We know we're loved by Him, and we know how much we need Him.

THE PRACTICE OF PRAYING

For much of my life as a follower of Jesus, I've heard that prayer happens when we talk to God, but that's only half of the truth. Over time, I've discovered that "to" should be replaced by "with." Prayer happens when we talk *with* God.

When we talk *to* God, we often carry our agenda into what amounts to a monologue. It makes no use of the pauses that are required in any relational space, and makes it feel transactional, rather than relational. It's so easy for anyone to reduce praying into something that's primarily me-oriented, but when we do so, we minimize the rich potential of everything God has to offer.

Talking *with* God is something altogether different.

When we talk *with* God, we remove any assumption that we already know the best answer. We enter into the Father's presence recognizing how needy we really are, so that "we may receive mercy and find grace to help in time of need" (Hebrews 4:16). When we talk with God, we do so with the full awareness that He probably has more to say than we do, and that we can surrender our perceived control into the hands of the only One who's already in control.

> **Praying is an intentional space where we**
> **communicate with God so we can hear His voice,**
> **experience the revelation of His character,**
> **and discover the heart of the Father.**

When we engage in the Practice of Praying, we intentionally place ourselves into a space that allows us to move away from the distractions that are all around us. In these sacred moments, we hear God's voice and discover His heart. When we pray more, we see more.

Embracing this reality creates great freedom to come to God, and to bring our hopes and expectations into His presence as often as possible.

So with this much at stake, it's easy to see why the enemy has so many different messages that pull us in the opposite direction.

"The details of my life are too trivial to bring to God."

"He doesn't really hear me anyway."

"He's already made up His mind, so why should I pray?"

"He doesn't understand my pain."

"God knows my heart, so why should I have to say it?"

"Prayer hasn't worked for me in the past, so why try now?"

"People will think I'm crazy if I claim to hear God's voice."

Notice that all of these voices have this in common: They're all spoken to us by our adversary to get us to doubt the goodness of the Father, and to call into question our standing in that relationship. That's why the Practice of Praying can be so difficult, especially at first — because there's someone standing against us. But thankfully, we can learn habits and disciplines that will help us discover this life-giving Practice.

DRILLS AND DISCIPLINES

The drills and disciplines of Christ followers throughout history might help serve as our guide. What they have all discovered in terms of walking intimately with Jesus can provide us with a great list of ancient but relevant connecting points. At the same time, these lists aren't exhaustive. We can learn new disciplines that might even work better for us. But regardless of the disciplines you choose, never forget that the goal of praying is to connect with the heart of the Father.

There are prayers we can pray before we eat a meal, with hearts full of gratitude for the provision before us, and the people around us. We can pray alone or with our family members before we go to sleep. We can pray The Lord's Prayer in gathered settings, and we can read the prayers of others in books and devotionals. We can write out our prayers. We can pray with our eyes open as we're standing on the sidelines of our kids' athletic events, as we're driving around, or as we're walking into a meeting. We can pray during the singing when we're gathered at church, or when we're listening to a portion of the sermon that seems to be speaking to us.

The Practice of Praying should also include lengthened and intentional space to communicate with God on a regular basis. Over the years, He's developed a pattern in my life that feels like breathing in, and breathing out — like inhaling, then exhaling. It's something that isn't rigid or bound by a certain order.

Reflect Quietly — I'll get away from anyone or anything else, close my eyes, and simply say, "Father, I love You, and I come into Your presence now." I'll inhale and exhale, and continue with some statements of gratitude. Our minds are noisy, and these statements help quiet them, so I can begin to hear the only voice that really matters. As things begin to quiet down, an aspect of God's character is often brought to the surface, and I'll just stay there, soaking it in. Other times, it's a situation in my life that comes to mind. It's like the Spirit saying, "This is what our conversation is going to be about today." Whatever agenda God sets for our time together, the habit of reflecting quietly allows Him to speak first, and helps me to begin a conversation *with* Him.

Share Transparently — We all come to God in need. We are needy people, and most of the time, that's the most transparent thing we can admit when we pray. I'll often simply tell Him, "God, I am in such great need of You," and then I share openly, and with vulnerability. God wants to hear about our struggles, our joys, and our pain. He loves to hear us confess that we're not in control. He delights in hearing us ask for His strength to help us break free from unhealthy life patterns. He also loves to hear us put previously unspoken words to the dreams we have for the next season of our lives. This is also the perfect time to say, "Help me to decrease so that You may increase."

Listen Expectantly — Next, I'll listen again. When we share transparently, it's often an outpouring of the heart, and we subsequently feel mercy and release. It can be emotional. As a dad, I've learned about the heart of the Father from my own children. They often come to me with something significant they need to talk about, and I'm able to bring a vantage point to their situation that they don't have. When they stop talking, I speak, and it's like that with God. Listening expectantly to God during these moments is of utmost importance, and His voice is often as clear as it'll ever be. For this reason, it's essential to remain in this dialogue, refusing to move on too quickly.

Receive Freely — Finally, simply receive whatever God is offering. It may be that we receive grace, mercy, love, or peace. We may also receive a challenge or a correction. We may also sense that there's someone we need to connect with, or something we need to do immediately. For me, this typically happens after I close my time of prayer, and may come throughout the day. But whenever it comes, receive it, respond to it, and allow it to transform your heart.

CONCLUSION

Practices are the spaces where we apply the correct information repeatedly. I encourage you to allow yourself to be inspired by a few of the habits mentioned here. Make a commitment to begin every day with time set aside for prayer. Don't make this mechanical or rote, but rather allow it to flow naturally. Don't be too worried about the order and don't be surprised if you cycle through various elements more than once. This is a conversation WITH GOD, after all. The important thing is to consider the opportunity to talk to your Father in Heaven and reflect, share, listen, and receive accordingly. Learn to admit your deepest needs, and to elevate your thinking about the priority of prayer.

As you walk through the doorway into the throne room of God, the door has already been opened because Jesus made the way. You're walking into the presence of great joy, great love, and great holiness. God is gracious, but He's also willing to rebuke. He's personal, and He's also glorious. So...

Reflect quietly.

Share transparently.

Listen expectantly.

Receive freely.

As you learn to talk with God, you'll discover the glory of His character that's being revealed, and the beauty of His heart that's on full display.

And never forget — He's in your corner.

CHAPTER 24

Learning

START HERE

SCAN TO WATCH

Living By *DESIGN* Rather Than Default

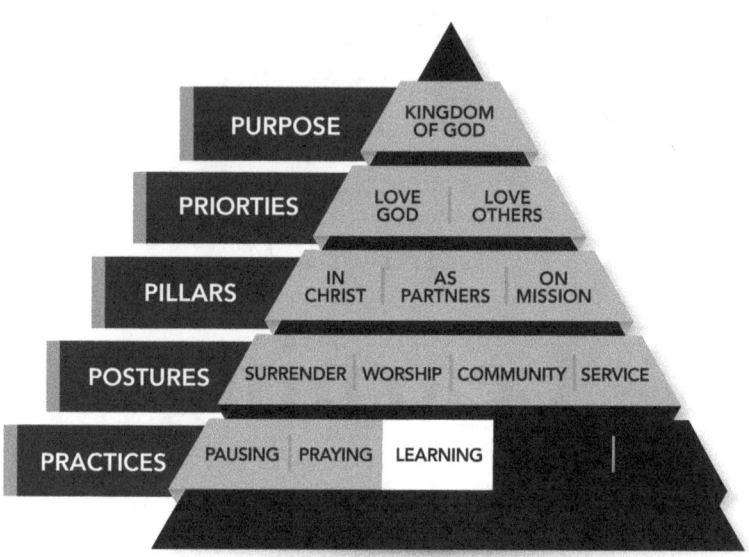

The most prolific quarterback and the greatest wide receiver in the history of the West Coast Offense actually played on the same team, at the same time. I had the unique privilege of not only hearing their stories from other players, but also of watching many of those stories unfold before my eyes.

It can be argued that Joe Montana was the best QB to ever play the game. Back in Chapter 8, I told you a story involving 22 Z-In — the offensive play that provides the foundational understanding for the West Coast Offense. At the height of his career, Joe Montana would be seen in meeting rooms, pencil and notepad in hand, still taking notes as Coach Walsh discussed 22 Z-In with the rest of the 49ers.

Montana's favorite wide receiver was Jerry Rice. When I played for the 49ers and was working out with the team in the offseason, I walked past the film room one day and noticed that Rice was watching game footage. At that exact moment, he was watching clips of Cris Carter (another Hall of Fame wide receiver in the NFL at that time). I was curious as to why Rice was watching film of other wide receivers so diligently, so I asked one of our coaches about it. Turns out, Rice worked with the 49ers film guy every single offseason to compile video clips of the top 10 wide receivers across the NFL from the previous season. He did this so that he could learn from them, even though his name was already at the top of that list.

People who have the greatest outcomes are resolute learners, all day, every day.

That's true for us too.

THE ESSENCE OF LEARNING

Learning entails an attitude of continual pursuit, not a mountain we climb and conquer. I believe the essence of learning begins as we live out the words of Moses that echo into our world today: "So teach us to number our days that we may get a heart of wisdom" (Psalm 90:12). Moses knew, and we must know, that the manner in which we approach *today* matters. When we get to tomorrow, today will be gone forever, and gaining a heart of wisdom is discovered as we lean into this truth. Learning is inextricably linked with a heart of wisdom.

Solomon wrote two books of the Bible — Proverbs and Ecclesiastes. In the latter, he repeatedly refers to himself in the original Hebrew as "Qoheleth," a term that English translations have rendered "convener," "collector," "preacher," or "teacher." Solomon tells us that he literally searched for everything under the sun, setting out to discover the meaning of all things. We know from another account that, when God asked him what his heart desired the most, Solomon asked for wisdom. God granted it to him (1 Kings 3:12), so he became the wisest human (apart from Jesus) to ever live. It's hard to miss the connection between being a lifelong searcher, and the wisdom he received from God. To desire a wise and discerning heart like Solomon is integral to living The 3:30 Life.

But where do we go to learn? Where do we discover the best source of information, and find the most powerful connecting narratives? The writer of Hebrews gives us the answer:

> *"Let us therefore strive to enter that rest, so that no one may*
> *fall by the same sort of disobedience. For the word of God is*
> *living and active, sharper than any two-edged sword, piercing*
> *to the division of soul and of spirit, of joints and of marrow,*
> *and discerning the thoughts and intentions of the heart. And*
> *no creature is hidden from his sight, but all are naked and*
> *exposed to the eyes of him to whom we must give account."*

Hebrews 4:11-13

In my playing days, I was given a printed playbook, and I was in that book every day, without exception. The better I knew it, the more prepared I was to fulfill my role on the team, and to best represent the desires of the coach while I was on the field. In the same way, the words of Scripture are the playbook for life. In its pages, we learn how to fulfill our role according to God's design, and to represent Him wherever we find ourselves. The Bible we hold in our hands is indeed "living and active" and "sharper than any two-edged sword."

> In doing so, we begin to see the difference
> between being smart and being wise.

The Practice of Learning

The Practice of Learning requires us to change the way we think — quite literally. Without this perspective change, we fall into a default life telling us that we've completed our learning once we get a college degree or achieve a certain status in our job. Throw fear, ambition, and pride into the mix, and it's easy to see why so many people simply quit the pursuit of learning. If the Practice of Learning helps to reinforce the Postures of The 3:30 Life, then we must choose it in order to live by design rather than by default.

When we engage in the Practice of Learning by God's design, we discover it's actually hardwired into humanity. God intended this so we might better understand the world around us. In doing so, we begin to see the difference between being smart and being wise. A smart person is about *Me*, but being a wise person is about *He*. A smart person *accumulates* knowledge, but a wise person *applies* the correct information. A smart person is only concerned with having a *set of facts*, but a wise person is far more concerned with having *the whole truth*. God has designed us to become increasingly righteous, not increasingly correct.

Learning is an intentional space where we discover the world as God designed it and we continue to grow over the course of our lifetime, so that we reflect Him in greater measure to a watching world.

Learning requires us to recognize our own limitations and finitude, and to look beyond ourselves. In the Practice of Learning, we discover, we grow, and consequently we display the glory of God into the world around us.

Learning prioritizes Scripture. When I studied at Stanford, there was an unspoken conviction that the highest form of learning took place in classrooms and research centers at elite universities around the world. Over the course of time, I've discovered that the study of God (commonly called "theology") is far and away the highest form of learning, and that all other information is designed to be held under its scrutiny. The more we learn about how God has revealed Himself, the more we learn about ourselves and about life as it's meant to be lived. First, the mind is instructed in the Word, then the heart is convinced, and finally it's put into practice.

Learning connects with other voices. Learning is a team sport, after all, and the voices of others represent people who are on our team. While individually we're eyewitnesses giving an account of the work of Jesus in our lives, we derive inspiration from the stories of others as well. At the same time, we are encouraged by the expert witnesses backing us up and affirming the bedrock realities on which we build our faith. We know that truth is on our side, and that our discovery of it involves voices outside of our own lives.

Learning involves our passions and interests. We should feel a great freedom to explore the things in life that we're passionate about, and that we find interesting or intriguing. As we expand our horizons and delve into new subjects and new hobbies, God takes those experiences and uses them as a relational bridge to others who are on a similar journey. We marvel about who God is when we push into our passions and interests.

THREE TYPES OF INFORMATION

In the Practice of Learning, it's all about information. There is no learning without information. Because we live in the explosive growth of the

Information Age, it's critical to not simply learn, but also to discern what information is valuable, and what is not. We must become wise discerners of what to apply our minds to. How we decide what to learn about, and what not to, is of eternal importance. In general, we all encounter three types of information:

1. **Harmful Information** — This is information we must *ELIMINATE* from our lives because it damages our hearts, and causes us to follow something or someone other than Jesus. Pornography, gossip, and all forms of injustice are examples of this, and must be removed.

2. **Irrelevant Information** — This is information we must learn to *MINOR IN*, not necessarily eliminate. It's one thing to give our minds a rest while escaping to our favorite TV series, but it's another thing when we allow our minds to atrophy as we stare blindly into the flatscreen over an entire weekend. When we make irrelevant things into our most relevant things, we can miss out on the opportunities that God is placing before us, and the people He's placing in our path.

3. **Relevant Information** — This is the information we must learn to *MAJOR IN*. Relevant information represents God's heart, and helps reveal His agenda. The primary source of this is God's Word, as revealed in Scripture. In The 3:30 Life, we learn to surrender our own agendas, as everything else becomes less enticing. As you'll discover, there's a rich and beautiful overlap here with the Practices of Pausing and Praying, because within those Practices, we receive God-inspired information that's relevant to the very life He's inviting us into.

DRILLS AND DISCIPLINES

When it comes to the ongoing habits and disciplines of learning, the wellspring runs deep with those who have gone before us. Whether it's formal learning in a university setting, or personal learning in solitude, followers of Jesus across generations offer us models of habits, drills, and disciplines that will help us see the world as God designed it. We should be inspired by them.

> We must discard any one-size-fits-all approach to learning, because there's no true universal measuring tool that says, "This is the level of intelligence I've achieved."

The most practical starting point for the Practice of Learning is discovering our learning type. Type the words "learning type" into your favorite search engine, and you'll immediately see there are a variety of ways to learn. Unfortunately, our education system doesn't always recognize this important truth, and instead measures learning by limited academic standards, i.e. tests like the SAT and ACT. Some of the most intelligent people we'll ever meet did poorly on those tests (or never took them), and don't necessarily have a diploma of any kind. We must discard any one-size-fits-all approach to learning, because there's no true universal measuring tool that says, "This is the level of intelligence I've achieved."

Some people learn in a group setting as a speaker presents a well-prepared monologue with notes and slides. Others learn better as they immerse their hearts and minds in a book, perhaps with a journal alongside. Because some learning involves other people, there are environments of group discussion where we interact with our peers (something we'll discuss with the Practice of Gathering). As children, we learned the value of experiential outings, and in the same way many adults find they learn best by doing.

As you begin to discover your learning style, you'll see that the sky really is the limit. No matter how your learning style is best represented, make certain to embrace the heart of learning at its core...

- **Be Curious** — Move through life with the full awareness that none of us already possesses a majority of the information available.

- **Be Inquiring** — Learn to ask good questions. Start sentences with phrases like, "What do you think about _____?" Listen closely to the answers.

- **Be Humble** — It takes a heart of humility to quit trying to be the smartest person in the room, and to just be quiet.

Conclusion

Are you ready to make the decision to become a lifelong learner? Are you ready to prioritize Scripture, and to embrace your design from God as someone who's been created to grow in your understanding of His world?

There's such great freedom here, and I pray you feel this freedom as you find your areas of passion and discover hobbies and interests around the things that intrigue you. Learn about traveling, or birds, or cooking, or landscape, or theater, or whatever's on your heart. Discover other voices through podcasts, books, videos, mentors, and documentaries. Give the Holy Spirit permission to show you the world by showing you the heart of others who share your passions and interests. Talk to other people and discover how they learn, and what they're immersing themselves in. Be resolute in discarding any harmful pool of information that's grieving the heart of God, and consequently affecting your relationships with others.

As you do so, you'll begin to reflect the character of God to a watching world. And make no mistake about it...

They really are watching.

CHAPTER 25

Gathering

START HERE

SCAN TO WATCH

Living By *DESIGN* Rather Than Default

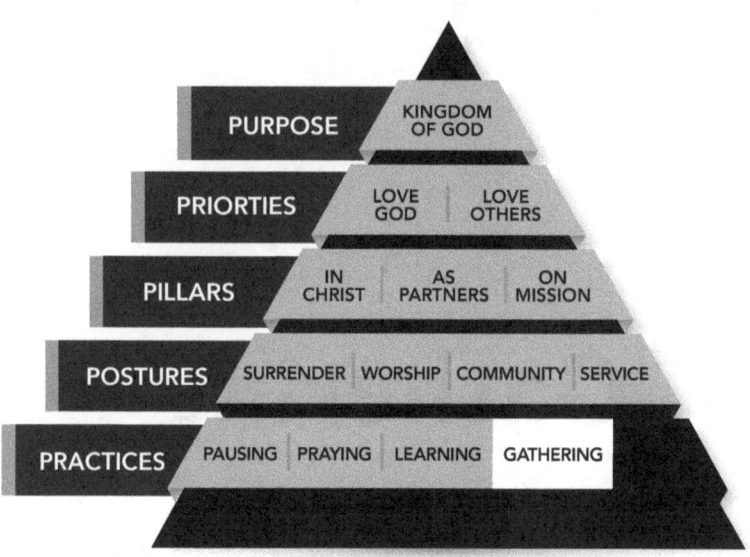

Practices are the spaces in which we identify and apply the correct information, time and time again, because the game is coming. Practices are often grinding and grueling, and those who commit to them will occasionally wonder if it's all worth it. In the middle of practice it's often hard to see if we're getting anywhere, and if all the effort is making any difference. Those who stick with it — those who persevere — know that breakthroughs come when we remain steadfastly dedicated to our regimens and routines.

Of all athletes, swimmers may endure the most rigorous and demanding practice discipline I've ever seen. My wife trained and competed in swimming through college and all three of our daughters have as well. The combination of time spent in training with the excruciating physical demand of that training is at a level few other athletes can relate to. So what makes it all worth the grind and discipline?

It's the breakthroughs.

Breakthroughs happen in a moment, but they've been earned well in advance through the toil of practice.

For swimmers, especially in shorter events like sprints, progress comes in tenths, even hundredths, of seconds. To swim a full second faster than ever before is a major breakthrough that always brings a smile to the face of the athlete.

I remember one such experience with my daughter Lindsay. She'd qualified for a big three-day competition held one year at the University of Texas in Austin. In the months leading up to it, her training had been focused on being as prepared as possible for the races she'd be competing in. As a matter of fact, *years* of her life had been dedicated to this sport she loved and to becoming the best version of herself possible, all to be ready for meets like this one.

After Day 1, it was clear Lindsay was "on," and one of her best events was coming up on Day 2 — the 100-yard backstroke. It's hard to capture the moment in writing, but watching Lindsay swim that race left a smile on her face so big that I still remember it to this day. She dropped more than a full second off her best time ever, eclipsing a standard that transitioned her from a great backstroker to an exceptional one. Lindsay experienced the kind of breakthrough that had kept her motivated and focused through all those long and difficult practice sessions.

We all want breakthrough moments, and we're profoundly thankful when they occur. The thing about breakthroughs, however, is that they don't just happen on their own. Though we don't know when they will come, we must expect them, hope for them, and prepare for them with dedication and discipline. That's what the Practices of The 3:30 Life are all about, and the Practice of Gathering just might be the one that triggers more breakthrough moments in our lives than anything else. God has wired us to be at our best when we are with others, and when others are with us.

THE ESSENCE OF GATHERING

Whether you're introverted and quiet, or extroverted and gregarious, everyone needs to spend time with other people. Some of the most enjoyable moments of our lives happen in our interactions with others, experiences marked by laughter, honesty, and deep connection. But if you're like me, it's easy to see how quickly the busyness of life can get in the way of pursuing important relationships with others. Fortunately, to help us, Scripture paints a motivating picture of people who are inextricably linked to one another, who recognize their need for one another, and who are better because of one another. Even though the Gospel changes us individually at first, we're unable to continue growing in isolation. We need people and people need us.

> "Let us hold fast the confession of our hope without wavering, for he who promised is faithful. And let us consider how to stir up one another to love and good works, not neglecting to meet together, as is the habit of some, but encouraging one another, and all the more as you see the Day drawing near."
>
> Hebrews 10:23-25

The writer of Hebrews highlights three core elements of The 3:30 Life, wrapping them together, and setting them in front of readers. Don't miss the powerful connection between the hope of Jesus, the faithfulness of God, and the necessity of being with other people — all experienced increasingly as we live every Today in light of That Day. Our need for other people is hardwired into our design by God Himself, and our experience of growth and hope is dependent on the ways we gather together. Solomon emphasized our need for one another when he declared, "And though a man might prevail against one who is alone, two will withstand him—a threefold cord is not quickly broken" (Ecclesiastes 4:12). He also expressed the refining effect of community: "As iron sharpens iron, so one person sharpens the other" (Proverbs 27:17 NIV).

But there's more.

In the Practice of Gathering, we begin to see the image of God in all people. When we spend time face to face with others, we discover them to be more like us than we ever thought, revealing the truth that the things we have in common far outweigh the things we don't. While our culture baits us into focusing on our differences, the narrative of Scripture invites us to see all people as being born imprinted with the image of God. "So God created man in his own image, in the image of God he created him; male and female he created them" (Genesis 1:27). The image of God in all people becomes a core tenet of why we gather, and as we do, we find community, commonality, and belonging. When we gather, judgment and generalizations about others break down, and we see more clearly God's handiwork in the lives of those He's created (Ephesians 2:10).

> Our need for other people is hardwired into our design by God Himself, and our experience of growth and hope is dependent on the ways we gather together.

THE PRACTICE OF GATHERING

We're inherently better when we're together. We've been created *for* community, and designed to be *in* community. We need others, and they need us, and that's why the Practice of Gathering is so vital to The 3:30 Life.

Gathering is an intentional space where we prioritize time with others, so that through those interactions we grow in Christ-likeness, and we see all people the way God sees them.

As we place ourselves into the spaces where gathering flourishes, it's not surprising to see that we grow in our love for God and for others. Our need to be together works as a virtuous cycle in our lives. Time invested with other people allows us to see God working beyond our own experiences, and reveals how much our lives mutually benefit one another. The result is a growing hunger that inspires us to initiate even more times of gathering. But as with every Practice, the difference between knowing the truth and acting on the truth will require both effort and sacrifice.

Gathering requires others on the same journey. In the Practice of Gathering, one key element is intentionally placing ourselves face to face with fellow Christ followers. While our goal is personal growth, there's also a collective attractiveness that's palpable, and full of hope. With the Practice of Gathering, we'll often feel compelled for others to experience the same thing. There's a consistent rhythm of *pulling into* our spaces of gathering so that we can *push out* into the world.

Gathering requires others outside of the faith. With all of the good happening when we gather with other Christ followers, it's tempting to develop a bunker mentality. But bunkering is not the same as gathering, and a life of isolation from the world at large isn't what Jesus had in mind when He told us to go into it (Matthew 28:18-20). God's invitation for us is to be relevant to the world without compromise, and to change the environment around us more than it changes us. So, while gathering with other Christ followers is a priority, we must also learn to gather with those who haven't yet chosen to follow Jesus.

Gathering requires commitment. The ongoing Practice of Gathering requires a commitment to be intentional with our calendars and our physical spaces. Even though we live in a digital age where virtual opportunities allow us to stay tethered to one another, a digital environment can only serve to augment our relationships, not replace them. There's no substitute for what happens in our lives when we engage with each other in our physical spaces of gathering. This is where we go beyond sharing the touch points and details of life, to dive deeply into relationships where we grow, where we're challenged, and where we receive grace and understanding.

> But bunkering is not the same as gathering, and a life of isolation from the world at large isn't what Jesus had in mind when He told us to go into it.

Gathering requires margins. In the Summer of 2007, our family spent more than a month traveling to South Africa and Tanzania. As we gathered with leaders throughout the area, I found myself getting uncomfortable with the amount of time we were spending in meetings. It felt like the participants never wanted to quit meeting. It soon became

apparent to me that they had learned a different cadence to their lives —
one that invited them to stay gathered until everyone was done talking.
One statement summed it up perfectly: "Steve, we often say around here
that in America everyone has watches, but no one has time. But in Africa,
no one has watches, and everyone has time."

My experience in Africa that summer prompted a personal reassessment
of the *urgent* and the *important*. I realized my life was full of 30- or
60-minute meetings with people, and my calendar revealed that they were
all back to back to back. I drove too fast, I was always a few minutes late,
and I was being lured into a culture that equates busyness with success. I
began to see the error of my ways and I sought steps to remedy it. I started
scheduling 90-minute meetings on my calendar, even though the other
person only planned for 60, and I was intentional about not being the
first person to say they had to leave. Other small steps like that allowed
me to stay gathered until everyone was done talking.

Without margin, we'll actually never meet with the people God intends
for us to spend time with. I assure you that the Practice of Gathering is
always the first to be pushed to the sidelines without proper margin in
our lives. The urgent will always overtake the important, and we'll miss
out on growing as God intends. Those around us will know that even
though we may be physically present with them, our minds will often
be miles away. There is eternal value in creating margin, and we must be
relentless in pursuing that.

DRILLS AND DISCIPLINES

When it comes to the habits and drills involved in the Practice of Gathering,
some will be organic and less defined, while others will be organized with

clear expectations. You'll discover, as I have, that both are always needed. First and foremost, we stand on what the Christian faith calls "fellowship." These are the intentional meetings we refer to as "church," and are centered around the Word of God and the person of Jesus. We gather in this manner regularly in order to receive truth, then to go into the world and give it away. But if the only place we gather is at church on the weekends, then we're missing out on God's full intent for our lives.

We can share a meal with others, placing our lives in the middle of theirs. The conferences and camps we attend will offer us some of the most profound and transformational moments of our lifetimes. We may join a small group Bible study, allowing our roots to grow deeper with God and others. Or we can meet one on one over coffee with a friend, just to connect. The list of options for gathering goes on and on.

It's important to remember that however you choose to gather, the goal is the growth that comes as a natural byproduct of time spent together.

CONCLUSION

As you look at your own life, is there a Christ follower you need to connect with? Is there someone outside the faith who'd love to hear from you? Is there an organized gathering you need to push yourself into, or a more informal connection with a friend just to catch up?

We've all been created to be with other people, and a life of following Jesus simply cannot be lived in isolation. What if it's *your* time to push past your fears, your excuses, and your overcrowded schedule? What if it's time to stand against any isolationist mentality that's developed over time, and instead choose to gather together again?

Transformation is the goal.

You need other people.

Other people need you.

God has designed you for this.

CHAPTER 26

Giving

START HERE

SCAN TO WATCH

Living By *DESIGN* Rather Than Default

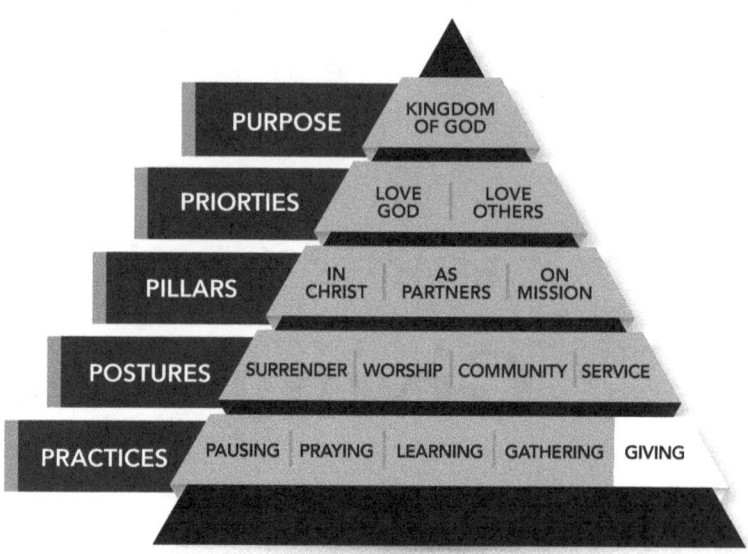

We've identified the Four Postures in The 3:30 Life — Surrender, Worship, Community, and Service. We've also made the case that each of these four Postures becomes more fully inflated when we press into God's design for our lives. Living like this requires practice on our part, which consists of various drills, routines, habits, and disciplines. The Practices we engage in every day become the fuel that God uses to breathe life into each Posture.

The fifth and final Practice of The 3:30 Life is Giving, and it's at the very heart of God.

The Essence of Giving

From age to age, God has always been the supreme example of what the heart of giving looks like. He is a Giver, and we don't need to look much further than the most popular verse in the Bible to see it: "For God so loved the world that *he gave* his one and only Son..." (John 3:16 NIV). It's been said that you can tell how much you love someone by what you're willing to give up for them. If that's the case, then humans are infinitely loved by God — a love on full display when God gave His one and only Son, so that He might have a forever relationship with us.

When it comes to our lives, Paul's words to a young pastor-in-training named Timothy capture the essence of giving:

> *"As for the rich in this present age, charge them not*
> *to be haughty, nor to set their hopes on the uncertainty of*
> *riches, but on God, who richly provides us with everything*
> *to enjoy. They are to do good, to be rich in good works, to*
> *be generous and ready to share, thus storing up treasure for*
> *themselves as a good foundation for the future, so that they*
> *may take hold of that which is truly life."*

1 Timothy 6:17-19

The command given to Timothy is meant to embed itself in our hearts. We learn that the antidote to selfishness and a Me-focused lifestyle is to cultivate a spirit of generosity. In addition, the reality of an eternal perspective is set before us — one that every Christ follower must become increasingly accustomed to, by faith. For when we give, any treasure we hope to receive is stored in another place, for another time, where the life we're all eternally designed for finally becomes a daily reality.

When we read about people who are "rich in this present age," he's not only talking about people in the top tier of wealth in our world. Chances are, if you're reading this book, he's talking about you too. For those of us who have a roof over our heads, and who eat more than one meal a day, we are by all global standards "rich."

This is also where the Practices of Praying and Giving overlap. When we ask God to "give us this day our daily bread" (Matthew 6:11), we're immediately confronted with three thoughts:

1. We're utterly dependent upon God to meet our needs.

2. We recognize He's given us provisions that go far beyond our basic needs.

3. We're invited to consider those who are waiting to have their needs met.

Consider this amazing thought: We might actually become the flesh-and-blood answer to others who are lifting up the same prayer. When we give, we're actually participating in a huge tapestry that God is weaving together behind the scenes. For me, and for so many others before me, participating in how God answers the prayers of others for "daily bread" increases the desire to be generous, while at the same time protects us from the hoarding and stockpiling we're all so prone to.

> For when we give, any treasure we hope to receive is stored in another place, for another time, where the life we're all eternally designed for finally becomes a daily reality.

The Practice of Giving trains us to make an accurate assessment of what we have, helping us experience yet another example of choosing He over Me by learning to live with less than we want, but still all that we need. By sowing into the needs of others, we actually become who we're truly designed to be. We emulate Jesus when we live generously.

The Practice of Giving

As we dive deeper into the Practice of Giving, Paul's letter to the Corinthians will help us chart a clearer path to generosity. Paul is writing to a specific group of people, but by the Holy Spirit, He's also writing to generations who would follow.

He's writing to you and me.

> "The point is this: whoever sows sparingly will also reap sparingly, and whoever sows bountifully will also reap bountifully. Each one must give as he has decided in his heart, not reluctantly or under compulsion, for God loves a cheerful giver. And God is able to make all grace abound to you, so that having all sufficiency in all things at all times, you may abound in every good work. As it is written,

> "'He has distributed freely, he has given to the poor; his righteousness endures forever.'

> "He who supplies seed to the sower and bread for food will supply and multiply your seed for sowing and increase the harvest of your righteousness. You will be enriched in every way to be generous in every way, which through us will produce thanksgiving to God. For the ministry of this service is not only supplying the needs of the saints but is also overflowing in many thanksgivings to God.

"By their approval of this service, they will glorify
God because of your submission that comes from your
confession of the gospel of Christ, and the generosity of your
contribution for them and for all others, while they long
for you and pray for you, because of the surpassing grace of
God upon you. Thanks be to God for his inexpressible gift!"

2 Corinthians 9:6-15

As we read passages like this, if we're not careful, we'll mistakenly interpret Paul's words with a "give money in order to get money" mindset, but that's simply not true. Throughout this entire passage, our "return" is rich, but it's not necessarily monetary. Instead, we read that we'll "abound in every good work," or that God will "increase the harvest of your righteousness," and all of it results in expressing "thanksgiving to God." Our return is seen in our character as we grow into the likeness of Christ.

Therefore, as it's revealed to us in Scripture...

**Giving is an intentional space where we release our
tangible resources to others, so that their needs are met,
and our God-designed potential is unleashed.**

God isn't asking us to give away the resources we don't have. The Practice of Giving invites us to release certain resources that God has *already* entrusted to us to become the answer to the daily bread prayers that others are praying at the moment. Doing so will result in our growth and increasing maturity in Christ. When we love others enough to sacrifice for them, this Practice has the effect of weeding the soil in our own lives (Matthew 13:1-23).

The Practice of Giving is about so much more than money. It's about faith, trust, love, and courage. Even though we might live with the fear of running out, we choose sufficiency over comfort, and we trust in the goodness of God.

The Perspective of Giving

When it comes to giving, many people adopt a perspective of scarcity, convincing themselves that their resources are on the brink of running out. American culture supports this idea and encourages us to work hard all of our lives to build into our retirement. We invest in proper savings strategies, retirement planning, and the like. Even though the concept of retirement isn't found in Scripture, we look forward to the day when we finally get to enjoy the accumulation of all that we've saved. While stewarding some of our money for later in life can be a good thing, it often quickly becomes an obsession, which removes our focus from the eternal view of stewardship we are called to honor.

God invites us into adopting a perspective of sufficiency, not scarcity. With eternity on the horizon, and with our focus remaining there, we discover a different timeline in play, and it's one we're invited to adopt and embrace with our whole hearts. The life that awaits us in heaven far surpasses our time on earth, and offers us a place to store our treasure where we can enjoy it forever.

Drills and Disciplines

Christ followers through the ages have given us practical disciplines that will help us engage in the Practice of Giving. Tithing to our local church, serving a hot meal to the hungry, or writing a monthly check to our favorite charity are just a few examples. Yet we should always be open to newer drills and disciplines as well.

We can always carry cash, and help remove the excuse of only having credit cards when a giving opportunity arises spontaneously. We can let others go first — in the grocery line, at the concert venue, or inside the coffeehouse. We can pay for the person behind us in the drive-thru, and we can give away the best spaces in the crowded parking lot on a blistering summer day. My wife Lori makes cards (with cash, a cross necklace, and the Good News of the Gospel inside) for our family members to carry with them — all as reminders of God's love, and a friendly smile to anyone in need that we might encounter throughout our day. These are just a few examples of how we can become positioned to practice giving at any moment.

Whether big or small, the Practice of Giving is about stepping into every opportunity as it arises.

CONCLUSION

It's something that became intensely personal to Lori and I during a Casting Crowns concert at Red Rocks Amphitheater, just outside of Denver, Colorado.

That's where we were first introduced to Compassion International. During the concert, their spokesperson invited us to "adopt" children in poverty by pledging to financially support them on a monthly basis. We took the step to support four — one to represent each of our four biological children. Later, we came to know some of the great people at Compassion, and they invited us to go on a vision trip with them. Soon after, in 2016, we went to Nairobi, Kenya. There we met two of the children and their families we'd been supporting financially over the past several years. In their homes, in the middle of the dirt and the desperation, we saw that *our* family's picture was on the wall of *their* home. We had become the answer to their prayers for daily bread, and it was one of the most impactful experiences of our adult lives.

On the way home from Africa that year, Lori gave me that look and said, "We're not leaving them in the slums." So in the coming months, we increased our giving to move them into an actual apartment building with solid construction and running water where they could begin to grow and flourish as a family.

We were simply stepping into the opportunity in front of us, and saying "yes" to God's invitation.

By the time the 2020 Pandemic shut down our world, I'd become friends with the CEO of Compassion International and our two ministries had begun to explore partnership opportunities together. He shared that during that exceptionally dark time, 70,000 of the Compassion children who lived below the line of extreme poverty were now at risk of not having even their most essential needs met. He shared the grim news with me that the majority of these children and their families would likely not survive the Pandemic. God broke my heart with this news and simultaneously filled my thoughts with the reality that 70,000 was the average number of seats in an NFL stadium. I began to pray that the Lord might move people to give in a way that would "fill" those empty stadium seats with those same vulnerable children, and provide for them along with their families. A few short weeks later, with the Lord at the helm, we ultimately partnered with Compassion on an initiative called "Fill the Stadium." Through the generosity of the pro athlete community and so many others, all of these children ended up receiving the ongoing support they needed to survive during the Pandemic.

Again, this is just one example where we were simply stepping into the opportunity in front of us, and saying "yes" to God.

Was it easy? Of course not. Did we have to place faith over fear? Countless times. Were we unsure of the outcomes? Absolutely. But we carried all of that uncertainty into our daily journey, and we just kept taking the next step, then the next step, then the next one.

You can take my word for it — start the Practice of Giving today, because it's an amazing journey. If you want to get off the sidelines and get into the game, start by releasing your tangible resources to others. God has already supplied His people with everything the world needs, and He's designed us to act as flowing rivers, not stagnant reservoirs.

We are not keepers. We are givers.

We are not entitled. We are grateful.

We are not stingy. We are generous.

And if the essence of love is truly bound up in giving...

...then what are we waiting for?

An End and a Beginning

START HERE

SCAN TO WATCH

Living By *DESIGN* Rather Than Default

This isn't the first time I've told you this, but it bears repeating — *you've come a long way!* Just think about where this journey has taken you...

In the first six chapters of the book, we walked through the foundations of The 3:30 Life. Long before we ever discussed what a follower of Jesus DOES, we discovered who that follower of Jesus really IS. Our Being always precedes our Doing, and we can't circumvent that order.

As we looked at John the Baptist, we observed a man who was fully aware of the assignment he'd been given by God, and how he consistently pointed people away from himself, and toward the only true Messiah. What John demonstrates, we can replicate, as we learn to move away from a life of Me, and move toward a life of He. As we quoted multiple times, the seven words from John must become our own:

"He must increase, but I must decrease."

John 3:30

The beginning of The 3:30 Life happens at the single greatest defining moment that I call The Great Exchange. Our response to God's invitation in that moment begins The Following, and opens the door to discovering the unique path He's chosen for us (Ephesians 2:10). We exposed the schemes of the defense, and discovered how the film room informs our strategies against him. At the heart of it all, the invitation from Jesus to "come, follow Me" is the one we must respond to.

Then, as we pressed forward, we learned how to live our lives by God's design, not by the world's default. This is where we learned how to authentically embrace the call to follow Jesus. It's also where The 3:30 Life Pyramid was introduced as a visual aid — a framework of understanding that can remain with you until the moment you see Jesus face to face.

At the pinnacle of the Pyramid is the single unifying Purpose we all have as followers of Jesus: the **Purpose** of the Kingdom of God. We learned that we can't ever experience that Purpose if we don't have the proper priorities, and so Christ's **Priorities** of loving God and others must become our priorities as well. We discovered that those Priorities are embedded in our lives via three reliable **Pillars** of being in Christ, as Partners, and on Mission. Underneath the Pillars, we identified the four **Postures** of all faithful Christ-followers as surrender, worship, community, and service. And finally, we learned how best to develop those Postures in our lives through the ongoing **Practices** of pausing, praying, learning, gathering, and giving.

After all that, here you are.

You may feel a little like I did when I got to this point in the writing process. On the one hand, there's a sense of accomplishment, completion, and fulfillment. This journey has proven to be about so much more than completing another task, or checking another box.

But on the other hand, you may feel a strong urge to look ahead, and ask yourself what's next? My hope all along has been that you'd read this book and feel inspired, and that your inspiration would lead you to follow Jesus more resolutely. This was never meant to be a book that you put on the shelf when you're done, never to open again. Instead, this has always been an invitation from a fellow player who's also a coach — an invitation to continue contemplating these concepts as a game plan for life, and even to share them with others.

If you and I lived in the same city, and if we were able to connect in person, I'd invite you to practice with me. During that time, I'd encourage you to push into the Four Postures with your whole heart. I'd ask you if surrender, worship, community, and service are present and growing in your life, and then I'd encourage you to invite two to three people who know you best to help answer that question as well.

At this point, I'd probably contemplate — together with you — if this isn't an end, but really a beginning? I can't tell you how many times God has brought me to the end of something, only to reveal that it was never really an end, but rather a turning of the page into a new chapter. That's when I'd invite you to go deeper in your Me to He journey during this next chapter of your life — to take the truths you've discovered in this book and apply them more intentionally each and every day going forward.

> Instead, this has always been an invitation from a fellow player who's also a coach — an invitation to continue contemplating these concepts as a game plan for life, and even to share them with others.

AND FINALLY...

All that we've discussed in The 3:30 Life has led to what I'm about to say next. The passage below from Matthew 25 is the exact thing my heart longs to hear from the God who created me to hear it. I pray it's the same with you. In this passage, Jesus paints a picture of the moment when we'll meet Him face to face, and chooses to do what He so often does throughout the Scriptures...

He tells a story.

> *"For it will be like a man going on a journey, who called his servants and entrusted to them his property. To one he gave five talents, to another two, to another one, to each according to his ability. Then he went away. He who had received the five talents went at once and traded with them, and he made five talents more. So also he who had the two talents made two talents more. But he who had received the one talent went and dug in the ground and hid his master's money.*

> *"Now after a long time the master of those servants came and settled accounts with them. And he who had received the five talents came forward, bringing five talents more, saying, 'Master, you delivered to me five talents; here, I have made five talents more.'*

> *"His master said to him, 'Well done, good and faithful servant. You have been faithful over a little; I will set you over much. Enter into the joy of your master.'*

> *"And he also who had the two talents came forward, saying, 'Master, you delivered to me two talents; here, I have made two talents more.'*

"His master said to him, 'Well done, good and faithful
servant. You have been faithful over a little; I will set you
over much. Enter into the joy of your master.'

"He also who had received the one talent came forward,
saying, 'Master, I knew you to be a hard man, reaping where
you did not sow, and gathering where you scattered no
seed, so I was afraid, and I went and hid your talent in the
ground. Here, you have what is yours.'

"But his master answered him, 'You wicked and slothful
servant! You knew that I reap where I have not sown and
gather where I scattered no seed? Then you ought to have
invested my money with the bankers, and at my coming I
should have received what was my own with interest.

"'So take the talent from him and give it to him who has the
ten talents. For to everyone who has will more be given, and
he will have an abundance. But from the one who has not,
even what he has will be taken away.'"

Matthew 25:14-29

We've all been entrusted with a treasure from God, and what we do with that
treasure has eternal significance. This is not a righteousness that earns us an
acceptable standing before God, as if that were even remotely possible. This is
a picture of what happens when the branches bear the life of the Vine (John
15:1-11). It's a powerful image of what it looks like when we complete the
assignment given to us since before the foundations of the world (Ephesians

2:9-10), after running the race marked out for us (Hebrews 12:1-3).
Use your imagination to envision this future moment — a moment that's both an end and a beginning — as God speaks His heart over you, and to you. I want you to hear those words that we all long to hear. It's difficult for me to express how badly I want this for you. At the end of your days, after all is said and done, I want you to hear...

"Well done, good and faithful servant. Enter into the joy of your master."

So go.

Go become the person who devoted the remainder of your life to everything He's entrusted you with.

Go run with perseverance, with your eyes fixed on Jesus.

Go become the person who lived your 3:30 Life, and who hears those words from God at the end of your days.

Go live every Today in light of That Day.

And may you — by the very same power that raised Jesus from the grave — be assured that this is the life YOU were designed for, and that you have everything you need to complete the work He's given you.

May you do it all for the glory of the One who created you, for the sake of the world.

Amen.

The 3:30 Life

Living By *DESIGN* Rather Than Default

For more resources visit:

www.the330life.com

Acknowledgments

Writing this book has been an unforgettable experience and there have been numerous times along the way when I wondered if it would ever be completed. I'm grateful for the way the Lord orchestrated the process and I'm abundantly aware of the incredible contribution so many others have made along the way. While I can't possibly thank everyone who has helped shape this book, there are a few I'm compelled to recognize as instrumental to producing what you hold in your hands.

At the very top of the list of those I want to thank is my wife, Lori. From the very beginning, when the idea of writing a book first emerged, you believed in me and encouraged me to faithfully complete what the Lord told me to do. I know it took many years and we both often wondered if and when it would come to fruition. I can definitively say that it never would have happened without your love, support and encouragement along the way. Thank you, Lori, for believing in me and for sharing this journey of life with me. Thank you for all the conversations we've had related to what I hope to convey to those who read The 3:30 Life, and for being my very first proofreader and editor. The wisdom and edits you brought to the process elevated the final outcome much like you have elevated me over all these years. Let's keep going and see what He has scripted for us from here. I love you and I love my life with you!

I'd also like to thank my family. Words fail to capture the incredible foundation and sense of confidence I feel from the love and support you provide. Though I try to express it, you can't possibly know how profoundly grateful to God I am for you and the depth of my love for each one of you. Thank you for all the ways you've each helped shape me into the person the Lord has designed me to be, and for the way you each follow Jesus passionately and live Kingdom-first lives. You inspire me more than you know, and so much of what I understand about the Father and His heart for people I've learned by being a part of this amazing family. I love you all and I'm always in your corner!

Next, to my partner in the writing process, Gary Molander. Thank you for knowing me so well and for the many years of creative collaboration. I'm grateful for your willingness and patience along the way to pull this book out of me. Your insights and questions sharpened the message, and you helped me find the words to express what was deep in my heart. Your relationship with Jesus is contagious and I love the way you pursue your 3:30 Life. You have truly been iron to me on this adventure and I'm humbled by the myriad of ways you've gone the extra mile to serve me in pursuit of this dream. Your friendship is a treasure to me and your partnership in seeing this through goes beyond words. Thank you Gary!

Though certainly included in the family acknowledgement as well, my son-in-law Matt Winaker played an instrumental role at the end of the writing process. Thank you Matt for carefully reading and reviewing each chapter, and suggesting edits and sharpening the message where it was needed. I love your relationship with Jesus and the wisdom with which you live life. This book is stronger because of your help and I'm grateful for you!

I'd also like to thank Aaron Sauer. It would be simple to say thank you for your creative genius and design expertise, without which this book would look and feel so very different. However, your collaborative participation in this book writing process has gone far beyond what people will experience as they enjoy the design and layout elements. Thank you for the extra time you invested in this project and your commitment to excellence. I am grateful for your friendship and humbled by the ways you served me along the way.

Thank you Jon Ackerman. I thought I understood the role of an editor and the necessity of one before writing The 3:30 Life. After working through this together with you, I can now see how much I failed to grasp. Your eye for detail, your mastery of writing protocols and your personal walk with Jesus proved pivotal in the finished product. Thank you for answering my many questions and guiding me through the writing process, along with meticulously editing each page. You are a tremendous partner and beyond that a trusted friend. Thank you!

To the entire team at Pro Athletes Outreach, thank you! It is one of the greatest joys and privileges of my life to serve Jesus together with you. Thank you for the significant and tangible ways you've each contributed to The 3:30 Life and it becoming a reality. Additionally, I'm aware of the equally profound and intangible ways I've grown in my walk with Jesus because of the time we've spent together serving His Kingdom purposes through this ministry. Thank you all for being faithful partners and may we all continue to pursue our unique designs together for as long as He has scripted.

Finally, to all The 3:30 Life readers. Thank you for the time you've spent reading these pages. I hope it has served you well in your pursuit of Jesus. He alone is the Author and He alone has crafted you uniquely to serve His Kingdom purpose. I have prayed for each of you without knowing who you are, that this book might be used by God to point you toward His design for your life and away from the default winds of life and culture. Thank you for pursuing Jesus and for inspiring others to do the same. Until we all meet on That Day...